O. J. Padel

ARTHUR
IN MEDIEVAL
WELSH
LITERATURE

University of Wales Press

Cardiff 2000

I

This book is about Arthur as a literary figure in medieval Wales. It is not about the Arthur of history, if there was such a person. It is widely assumed that the legendary figure was derived from a historical one, but it is equally possible that the seemingly historical Arthur was created by the historicization of a figure of legend. The legendary figure of Arthur was remarkably consistent in local British folklore for over a thousand years, from its first appearance in the ninth century to folklore current in the nineteenth; but learned authors, the intermediaries through whom we have received our knowledge of early Welsh traditions, sometimes gave their own interpretations of the character – either for their own reasons or because they knew of Arthur's wider literary reputation – rather than giving a close portrayal of the traditional figure. For this reason it is essential, when studying the portrayal of Arthur in a particular text, to try to understand the nature and purpose of that text; yet the understanding of individual texts is naturally a subjective matter. The nature of the literary works therefore receives particular attention in the pages which follow, even though space here cannot allow for all the different interpretations that have been offered of some of the better-known texts.

Wales has no monopoly of the Arthurian legend. Although the earliest mentions of Arthur are found in the ninth-century Welsh-Latin HISTORIA BRITTONUM ('The History of the Britons'), he also occurs in similar contexts in Cornwall, southern Scotland and Brittany, as soon as there are records of a kind liable to show the local folklore which was his particular domain. For our purpose the important point is not whether he was based on a historical person (for no records survive capable of answering that question), but the fact that in the early Middle Ages, by the twelfth century at the latest, he was renowned in local storytelling wherever Welsh and its sister languages were spoken.

II

The Earliest Texts

The earliest datable text mentioning Arthur is in Latin, the HISTORIA BRITTONUM formerly attributed to Nennius. This was probably compiled in north Wales in the years 829–30. It is worth recalling, in passing, the notable absence of Arthur from an earlier Latin work, Gildas's DE EXCIDIO BRITANNIAE ('On the Ruin of Britain'), composed in the sixth century. Gildas gave a historical summary of the English takeover of Britain, and if Arthur had played a major part in the British resistance we might well have expected Gildas to name him, as he does Ambrosius Aurelianus. Likewise, Arthur is absent from Bede's ECCLESIASTICAL HISTORY OF THE ENGLISH PEOPLE, written about a century before the HISTORIA BRITTONUM, though in Bede's case other reasons for his silence might be envisaged.

Given that the HISTORIA BRITTONUM, dating from the ninth century, is the earliest Arthurian text, its most striking feature is that it contains two different, seemingly contradictory, portrayals of Arthur. One is the often-quoted 'List of Arthur's battles against the English', where Arthur is depicted as the great military leader (*dux bellorum*) who led the British kings against the second generation of English settlers. (The context seems to imply that Arthur was not regarded as a king himself.) Twelve battles are specified, at nine sites (four at a single site). The identification of place-names in early documents is dependent upon the context, and this list supplies so little context that safe identification is impossible for the most part; this has made the list a rich quarry for those wishing to locate Arthur in their own particular areas, wherever those may be.

The final battle, Mount Badon, probably in southern England, is no doubt the one named by Gildas – who, by implication, attributes the victory instead to Ambrosius Aurelianus. A few other battle sites are also recognizable from Welsh legend: that at the 'River Bassas' recalls Baschurch in the Welsh Marches, named in the *englyn* poetry concerning Heledd; that at the 'city of the Legion' sounds like the seventh-century battle of Chester where thousands of monks of Bangor were said to have been slaughtered. The only sites also named elsewhere as battles involving Arthur are Badon (also in the Welsh Annals, see p. 10) and the River Tryfrwyd (*Tribruit*): Arthur's opponent there, we learn from the poem 'Pa ŵr yw'r porthor?' (see p. 29), was the legendary Gwrgi Garwlwyd ('Man-hound Rough-grey'), who used to *slay a corpse of the Welsh every day, and two on Saturdays so as not to kill on a Sunday*, according to the Triads; he was eventually killed, though not by Arthur, in one of the 'Three Fortunate Assassinations'.

For most of the battles no detail is given, only the names, which may have been all that the author of the HISTORIA knew of them. The more interesting battles are those where further information is given, and at these points the account begins to acquire a legendary, rather than historical, tinge: at the battle of the 'fort of Gwynnion' Arthur *carried the image of the Virgin Mary on his shoulders*, put the pagan

4

English to flight and achieved a great slaughter of them through the assistance of Christ and Mary. At Badon he personally killed 960 men in a single onslaught. The author hints at darker days to come, saying that Arthur was victorious in all his battles (he carefully avoids mention of the final battle at Camlan), and that his successes prompted the English to seek further support from their kinsmen on the Continent: the implication, not stated, was that after Arthur's day the English again extended their dominion.

The whole passage thus has a legendary quality to it, and the suggestion that it is based upon a Welsh poem, with rhymes appearing in the names of some battles, has found widespread acceptance. However, Charles-Edwards has pointed out that earlier in the HISTORIA a similar list of four battles against the English (only three named), attributed to Vortimer (Gwrthefyr), son of Vortigern, shows no sign of any rhyme-scheme, although it too has a legendary context. If the Arthurian battles were taken from a lost poem, we should expect to find comparable poems in surviving Welsh literature: according to preference, we could envisage it as similar either to that attributed to Taliesin in praise of Cynan Garwyn, the sixth-century king of Powys, listing his successful battles throughout Wales and in Cornwall, or to the legendary Arthurian poem 'Pa ŵr yw'r porthor?', to be discussed below (pp. 26–32), listing the achievements of Arthur and his warriors. Evidently between the time of Gildas in the sixth century and the writing of the HISTORIA in the ninth, Arthur had become a leading figure of the British resistance in Welsh legend. This makes it odd that he was not named in the earliest prophetic poetry as a leader who would return to fight the English (see pp. 61–2).

The List of Battles provides the context for another early reference to Arthur, which may well be the earliest Welsh text naming him: the line in the GODODDIN which praises one hero, Gwawrddur, for his achievement in providing food for black crows or ravens on the wall of a fortress, *though he was not Arthur* (*gochore brein du ar uur caer, ceni bei ef Arthur*). The date of this line cannot be ascertained with assurance, since both the date of the GODODDIN poetry generally and the date of individual lines within the corpus are open to debate. It can with some safety be assumed that the line goes back to the eleventh or tenth century, perhaps earlier; so it need not necessarily pre-date the references in the HISTORIA BRITTONUM, though it could be of around the same period.

This line of praise is to be understood as an example of the grim understatement which the GODODDIN often uses as a poetic device for praising its heroes; a few lines earlier a *son of Golystan* (*mab Golistan*) is praised for his valour in attack, *though he was not leader* (*cen nei bei guledic*), recalling Arthur's description as military leader in the List of Battles. The author of the praise of Gwawrddur, in making the comparison with Arthur, may have been thinking of Arthur's legendary single-handed slaughter of hundreds of Englishmen. The comparison, therefore, has no bearing on the question of Arthur's historical existence. Most heroes named in the GODODDIN are treated in a sober and factual manner; but this mention, more of a non-mention, is of a different kind, closer in mood to the refrain which

6

recurs in the GODODDIN, *Out of three hundred only one (or three) returned,* with its similarly legendary quality. (Compare also the refrain, *Three ship-loads we went; only seven men returned,* in the poem 'Preiddiau Annwn'; see pp. 34–5.) This allusion to Arthur in the GODODDIN accords with the more legendary dimensions of the battle-list in the HISTORIA BRITTONUM.

The other reference to Arthur in the HISTORIA is at first sight of a different kind from the battle-list. As an appendix the HISTORIA contains a list of the Wonders of Britain – wonders such as the hot springs of Bath, an altar of St Illtud suspended in mid-air with no visible support, and the sixty islands, each with an eagle's nest, in Loch Lomond. Two of these wonders were associated with Arthur. One of them was a stone bearing the footprint of Arthur's hound, Cafall, which left its imprint there when hunting *the pig Troyt.* The stone was located on top of a cairn, on a hilltop (now Corn Gafallt) near Rhaeadr. If the stone were removed from the hilltop it would find its own way back to the cairn. The other wonder was a tomb in Ergyng, again in the Welsh Marches, located beside a spring called *Licat Amr* (Llygad Amr, 'the eye or spring of Amr': *llygad* ('eye') also means 'source of a stream'). In this legend, the name Amr was supposed to refer to a man, though actually it is probably a river, the one now called Gamber in Herefordshire. Amr was said to be the son of Arthur, who had been killed by Arthur himself and was buried in the tomb – hence the local name. The tomb was of variable length, never twice the same, *and I myself have tested it,* the author tells us.

In these wonders the text recounts local legends,

linked with place-names. The fact that both are located in the mid-Welsh Marches need not be significant: this could be due to the author's sources of information, and we may legitimately envisage similar legends elsewhere in Wales, and further afield too. Such legends are common at later dates, as we shall see. Of Arthur's killing of his own son, presumably without recognizing him as in stories from other cultures, nothing more is known. But the earlier wonder is of significance since it shows that the hunting of the magical boar Twrch Trwyth, the climax of the Arthurian story 'How Culhwch won Olwen', was already known, and located in the Welsh Marches, in the earlier ninth century. In the later tale the location of the hunt is different; but it is to be expected that such stories were relocated at different sites, according to whatever suited different storytellers. (For the name of the Twrch Trwyth, later poetry used the form *Trwyd*, in keeping with the form *Troit* found here, rather than *Trwyth*: see p. 59. It seems that the form *Trwyth* found in CULHWCH is aberrant; but it is now established by frequent modern usage.) The other significant feature of the wonder is the name of Arthur's dog, Cafall ('horse'). This name recurs in CULHWCH, both for Arthur's dog and for a horse (not Arthur's), and again for his dog in the romance of GERAINT; the implication of the name, that the dog was of enormous size, conforms with later hints that Arthur himself was a giant.

Although these two wonders seem to belong in a very different world from the military campaign of Arthur's twelve battles, that is so only if we try to read the battle-list as a historical record. If we observe instead the legendary dimensions of that list, then the two passages have more in common.

However, the continuing Arthurian tradition, in Welsh and other literatures, was itself often split between trying to fit him into known history and acknowledging the magical and legendary quality of his world; so we may view this duality in the earliest Arthurian text as establishing the pattern for all later Arthurian literature. During the main period of Arthur's literary fame (twelfth to fifteenth centuries) the HISTORIA itself was not widely read, but it had an extensive indirect influence through the popularity of Geoffrey of Monmouth, who drew upon it in writing his own HISTORY OF THE KINGS OF BRITAIN, completed in about 1138. It is reasonable, therefore, to consider that the twofold image in which we view the figure of Arthur, both historical and legendary, has been perpetuated from the ninth-century HISTORIA through to the later Middle Ages, and thence down to the present day.

It is possible that there is a third, indirect, allusion to Arthur in the HISTORIA. Within the story of St Germanus and his work converting Britain to Christianity, there is an episode in which the saint visited a wicked tyrant in Powys, Benlli (*Benli*), known elsewhere as Benlli Gawr ('Benlli the Giant'). This sinful ruler refused hospitality to the saint, who accordingly destroyed Benlli and his fortress in a night-time incendiary display. A reference by the thirteenth-century poet Bleddyn Fardd to his patron as being *gwaewddur ual Arthur wrth Gaer Uenlli* ('spear-harsh, like Arthur against Benlli's Fortress') suggests that Arthur had played a part in an attack against this same tyrant. However, there is no certainty that Arthur's involvement in the attack on Benlli was claimed as early as the ninth century.

In the GORCHAN ('additional or long song'?) of Cynfelyn, a longer hero's lament transmitted alongside the GODODDIN poetry, the phrase *torch trychdrwyt* occurs, apparently as a comparison for the hero Cynfelyn. Although obscure, this phrase may contain a reference to the Twrch Trwyth (properly *Trwyd*, as noted above); if so, it presents another legendary character in this body of poetry, to place alongside the comparison made with Arthur in the GODODDIN itself. This further allusion to the Arthurian story, if such it is, might be of about the ninth or tenth century.

One last text belongs in this same group of the earliest allusions to Arthur. It is again one written (mainly) in Latin, though by a Welshman who was not averse to using his own language for occasional phrases or literary allusions. The Welsh Annals (ANNALES CAMBRIAE) were probably compiled in south Wales in the tenth century, though the earliest manuscript is of about 1100 and has received additions made in the intervening two centuries. Since this earliest text of the Annals appears in a manuscript alongside the earliest surviving text of the HISTORIA BRITTONUM (as well as Welsh genealogies), the two may have cross-fertilized each other.

The Annals contain two references to Arthur. Under the year 516 the *battle of Badon* is named, *in which Arthur carried the cross of Christ for three days and nights on his shoulders, and the Britons were victors.* A few entries later, in 537, occurs the earliest reference to *Gueith Camlann*, the battle of Camlan, *in which Arthur and Medrawd died.* The earlier entry is obviously connected in some manner with the similar legend in the earlier List of Battles of Arthur carrying the image of the Virgin Mary on his shoulders at the battle of Gwynnion; yet neither can be derived from the other, since the discrepancies between them are too great (Gwynnion instead of Badon; the image of the Virgin instead of the cross of Christ – is the latter supposed to be an image or replica?). It would seem that both texts were drawing upon a legend which had already assumed variant forms; but they agree in ascribing the victory at Badon (apparently incorrectly) to Arthur. It has been suggested that Arthur's carrying the two religious burdens *on his shoulders* is an error for *on his shield*, through written confusion between *ysgwyd* ('shield') and *ysgwydd* ('shoulder'), words often associated in early poetry (*iscuit* and *iscuid* in Old Welsh spelling). However, it seems unlikely that the same error would have been made twice by Welsh-speakers in transmitting a known legend; nor do we have other mentions of pictorial representations on shields from early Welsh culture. It is possible that 'shoulders' was always intended.

The second Annal entry is of interest for presenting the battle later famed as Arthur's last, and the character of Medrawd (Mordred in later medieval literature), Arthur's nephew and betrayer; however, it is not made clear here that Arthur and Medrawd were on opposing sides. Geoffrey of Monmouth, in the 1130s, located this battle in Cornwall; but he seems to have had his own reasons for associating Arthur very closely with Cornwall, and he was alluding to the name of the River Camel, which actually has a different derivation. Again, because of the lack of context in the Annals, there is no way of telling whether this battle was thought to be located in Wales (where there are at least two known places

11

called Camlan), or further north, like some other locations mentioned in the Annals, or indeed elsewhere.

The Annal entries, even in the earliest text, include several which must have been made retrospectively – such as the births of St Brigid, St David and St Columba – and others which seem legendary, such as the death of Bishop Ebur at the advanced age of 350 years, and the deaths of Gwrgi and Peredur, sons of Eliffer, in 580. The Annals place *Gueith Cair Legion*, the battle of Chester, in the year 613, almost a century after their first mention of Arthur. As historical sources the Annals and the HISTORIA tend to cancel each other out, because of their inconsistencies; but as literary sources they serve, together with the allusion in the GODODDIN, to give us a picture of the Arthurian legend in the ninth and tenth centuries. Arthur was a military leader of legendary prowess, capable of felling 960 men single-handedly in one attack, and using Christian symbols to aid his fight against the pagans; he was also associated with local landmarks – a rock where his dog left its pawprint, a redoubtable boar which he hunted, the mysterious tomb of his son whom Arthur had himself tragically killed. These two aspects, the military and the legendary, really belong together. Most seekers after the 'historical Arthur' choose to ignore the legendary aspect; but if the two are to be separated, then other early evidence from outside Wales (see chapter VII), combined with Gildas's silence about Arthur, shows the Arthur of local legends and magical animals as the dominant one until the twelfth century, when the military Arthur became more prominent. We might see this contrast as one between folk legends (magical

12

animals) and literary traditions (Arthur the soldier); but it may be preferable to see them as two complementary aspects of the hero.

Arthur's World: Culhwch and 'Pa ŵr yw'r porthor?'

We cannot know what quantity of Welsh Arthurian material, oral or written, prose or poetry, from the Middle Ages has been lost: all we can do is extrapolate from what survives. But two texts seem almost designed to provide an overview of Arthur and his literary world, containing allusions and flashbacks to a range of additional events in which Arthur and his men played a major role. So we can be confident that there was a body of now-lost stories, written or oral, which the audiences of these two texts were expected to recognize. However, the texts do not tell us a great deal about the character of Arthur himself. In contrast with the Four Branches of the Mabinogi, where individual characters emerge distinctively through their actions and words, Arthur's character does not seem to have been a major concern of storytellers and poets, to judge by the extant material.

The two works which provide so much information are the prose tale, MAL Y KAUAS KULHWCH OLWEN ('How Culhwch won Olwen'), found in the White Book of Rhydderch and the Red Book of Hergest among the other tales known nowadays as 'The Mabinogion'; and the untitled poem in the Black Book of Carmarthen, known from its opening words *Pa gur* ('Pa ŵr yw'r porthor?', 'What man is the gatekeeper?'). Like almost all medieval Welsh literature, these texts cannot be dated precisely, but they are likely to be rather older than the manuscripts in which they survive, which are of the thirteenth century (Black Book), the fourteenth (White Book) and *c.* 1400 (Red Book). Current thinking would place both texts around the year 1100, while acknowledging that both, particularly the prose tale, could have received minor additions or alterations in copying after that date. The particular significance of the date, even though it is uncertain, is that it is earlier than Geoffrey of Monmouth's HISTORY OF THE KINGS OF BRITAIN (completed in about 1138), since knowledge of that work formed the great watershed of Arthurian literature, in Wales as elsewhere.

The plot of the prose tale is the assistance of Arthur and his men given to Arthur's nephew Culhwch, to enable him to win as his bride Olwen, daughter of the giant Ysbaddaden, overcoming the impossible conditions set by the giant – a classic folk tale, but here expanded far beyond its normal scope. The chief task, providing the climax of the tale, is the hunting of the formidable magical boar, Twrch Trwyth.

Both works, CULHWCH and 'Pa ŵr yw'r porthor?', adopt similar devices for alluding to other stories and thus widening their frames of reference. In CULHWCH Arthur's gatekeeper on New Year's Day, Glewlwyd Gafaelfawr ('Bold-grey Mighty-grasp'), wishing to convey vividly the splendour of the stranger (Culhwch) waiting at the gate, reminisces about adventures which he has shared with Arthur:

Two-thirds of my life has passed, and two-thirds of yours. I was [with you] *in Caer Se and Asse, in Sach and Salach, in Lotor and Fotor, in Greater and Lesser India. I was in the battle of the two Ynyrs, when the twelve hostages were brought from Scandinavia. I was in Europe, in Africa, in the islands of Corsica, and in Caer Brythwch and Brythach and Nerthach. I was there when you killed the warband of Gleis son of Merin, and when you killed the Black Beast son of Dugum. I was there when you conquered Greece in the east. I was in Caer Oeth and Anoeth, in the Caer of Nefenhyr of the Nine Teeth. Fair lordly men we saw in those places, but I have never seen a man as handsome as him who is now at the gate.*

Some of the adventures mentioned by Glewlwyd are known from other sources, and they have points in common with a Welsh poem which recounts the Conquests of Alexander, an international literary legend in its own right. Other adventures are unknown elsewhere, and may have been invented by the author purely for rhetorical effect (*Lotor and Fotor*), so as to display his own learning or verbal dexterity. The result is a combination of the two aspects of Arthur found in the earliest texts: military exploits, here embracing the known world from Scandinavia to Africa and Asia, and struggles with a supernatural element, here against fearful creatures (the Black Beast, Nefenhyr of the Nine Teeth).

The same impression is provided more fully by another rhetorical passage in the tale, the list of warriors of Arthur's court, whose names Culhwch invokes in order to press his demand for Arthur's assistance. The list starts off reasonably enough, with Cai and Bedwyr, Arthur's usual companions in medieval Welsh literature, but rapidly gains a momentum of its own as the author again takes the opportunity to show off his learning and verbal prowess, with punning, alliteration, allusions to other stories which may or may not have existed and references to characters from other domains, all of a quality intended to amaze us by their dexterity or sheer bravado, such as three different kings of France (including Gwilenhin, who sounds suspiciously like William the Conqueror: our author is unlikely to have been worried by the fact that William the Conqueror never was king of France, if he even bothered to think about it); several Irish heroes including Cú Chulainn, Conchobhar mac Nesa, and Fergus mac Roich; various monsters, giants, saints and figures from mythology such as Manawydan son of Llŷr, as well as a number of characters associated elsewhere with Arthur. The overall total is 225 individuals (including some repetitions), plus twenty ladies of Arthur's court. In describing these characters the author makes several references to Arthurian stories, once again either military exploits (chiefly Camlan, the only battle of Arthur's named in the tale) or combats against fearsome animals.

One of the remarkable features of the list, for all its length and its surprising inclusions, is the omission of certain names. Medrawd, whose name had been linked with Arthur's since perhaps the tenth century (the Welsh Annals), and was to be linked with it again in the twelfth by both Geoffrey of Monmouth and the court poet Gwalchmai ap Meilyr, is absent; so are Arthur's son Amr, known from the ninth-century HISTORIA BRITTONUM, and another son Llachau, known both from later court poetry and from the *englyn* poetry and 'Pa ŵr yw'r porthor?'; so, too, is Arthur's nephew Eliwlad, known from the dialogue 'Arthur and the Eagle' (see pp. 64–5). All of these characters are thus associated with Arthur in earlier or near-contemporary texts, and might have been expected to be named in a list of the warriors of Arthur's court.

Correspondingly, we should not suppose that all the men and women named in the list were regular members of Arthur's company. The author was here indulging himself on the theme of Arthur's band of warriors, for the sake of virtuosic display. Similar, but much shorter, lists occur in other texts (discussed below), notably GERAINT and THE DREAM OF RHONABWY, and (in the fifteenth century) the triadic 'Twenty-four Knights of Arthur's Court'. Although all these texts are later than CULHWCH in date, the idea of Arthur's band of companions was presumably much older, as is the ninth-century list of his battles, and the author of CULHWCH was playing with the concept. A recital of Arthur's companions is likewise the central theme of the poem 'Pa ŵr yw'r porthor?' (see below).

Before considering the portrayal of Arthur himself in CULHWCH, we need, therefore, to establish the nature of the text itself. Its chief literary characteristic is its humorous light-heartedness, and one major element of that is its exuberant extravagance. The humour has been described as 'irony', but it is unclear which sense of that complex word could be applied to the tale, and much of the humour – incongruous exaggeration, verbal virtuosity and knockabout slapstick – is as far removed from the subtle understatement of irony as any humour can be. The author delights particularly in giving twists to well-known themes, whether by exaggeration or by the addition of an element. The overall tone is set from the start, when the widely used motif of a plant growing on a loved

18

one's grave is distorted, so that the king, Culhwch's father, has his wife's grave checked daily in the hope of finding a bramble so that he can remarry. When the moment comes the chosen bride is unfortunately already married: the husband is killed off in a flash, his lands seized, and the new queen taken home, leading straight into the Wicked Stepmother theme. The directness of action, literary playfulness and childlike lack of responsibility shown in this episode all recur throughout the tale.

Another example of such a distortion is the extension of the list of impossible tasks stipulated by the giant (the *anoethau*, 'marvels'), from their usual three in number to forty, including the formidable Twrch Trwyth himself, hunted for the comb and shears sitting between his ears in order to dress the giant's hair for the wedding. A third such alteration occurs in the theme of the Helpful Animals, when a nest of ants saved from a disastrous fire performs one of the giant's tasks by collecting every flax seed previously sown by him: the addition, unique to this version, is that a single seed seemed to be missing, but was brought in late by a lame ant. The presence of so many imaginative elaborations of well-known themes suggests that they were mostly inserted by the author of the tale for his own exuberant purposes, in order to show off his virtuosity and wit, just as the list of Arthur's warriors enables him to show off his verbal prowess. These elaborations make it hard to generalize about the Arthurian legend from CULHWCH alone, for one is never sure whether a particular feature appearing in the tale would also have occurred in other stories at the time, or was due to the author's own inventiveness.

The unexpected twists in CULHWCH also raise the question of whether the tale should be regarded as a parody, of either a folk tale or (if not the same thing) an Arthurian tale; however, to regard it thus may be to impute over-literary intentions to the author. Not all instances of exaggeration in literature are necessarily conscious parodies. In this context, it is instructive to compare a late medieval text which is actually a parody of CULHWCH itself, ARAITH IOLO GOCH ('Iolo Goch's oration'). This short rhetorical sketch does not mention Arthur, but it contains verbal echoes of CULHWCH, even near-quotations, including references to the battle of Camlan. Its brevity, deliberately inconclusive ending and echoes of CULHWCH all clearly show it to be a parody, and it can profitably be compared with THE DREAM OF RHONABWY (see pp. 96–9); but CULHWCH itself is not so readily classified. Its wide-ranging playful inventiveness may include parody, but the author's aim in CULHWCH was to entertain and show off, rather than to make a literary comment about other texts. To appreciate his achievement the text needs to be enjoyed aloud: of all the Mabinogion it is the one which loses most by being read silently, or in translation.

From all this it will be clear that it would be misguided to think of Arthur's world in CULHWCH as a 'heroic' one; at best it is so only in the loosest sense of that term. The true heroic ethos, finely displayed in the GODODDIN, with its warrior nobility willing to stand hopelessly against overwhelming odds for the sake of their honour and their ruler, is far removed from the no-holds-barred cunning of the folk tale, typically illustrated in CULHWCH. Cai and Bedwyr cram Dillus the Bearded into a specially dug pit, so as to pluck out his beard in safety – and then they kill him anyway, to avoid any risk of reprisal. To be sure, Arthur then offends Cai greatly by taunting him for their cowardice; but a concern for reputation can be found in many types of literature apart from the strictly heroic. The encounters of Arthur's men with Wrnach the Giant (tricked of his own sword, because it was one of Ysbaddaden's demands, and then killed with it) and with the Very-Black Witch, degenerating into an unseemly scuffle until Arthur ends it by chopping her in half, are conducted in a manner which is typical of the folk tale, but very different from the heroic atmosphere of the GODODDIN.

The chivalric code of the late medieval romances is different again, though it has significant points in common with both the heroic and the folk-tale ethos (see p. 92). Interestingly, Arthur seems to fore-shadow that later code, and the plots of many later romances, when he sums up the custom of his court in CULHWCH, saying, *Ydym wyrda hyt tra yn dygyrcher. Yd ytuo mwyhaf y kyuarws a rothom, mwyuwy uyd yn gwrdaaeth ninheu ac an clot ac an hetmic* ('We are nobles as long as we are sought out: the greater the bounty we may give, the greater our nobility, fame and honour'). The literary recognition of generosity as a virtue, like the regard for honour, is of course not confined to heroic societies. But for the most part the atmosphere of the story remains that of the folk tale, with its moral simplicity of goodies and baddies, and the unhesitating, heartless disposal of the latter by any means available.

However, this heartless tone raises another import-ant question: whether there is also a serious side to the story. So pervasive is the humour that there is scope for uncertainty; but the author expertly varies the pace, doubtless to keep his audience's interest lively, and some places can be suggested where the humour does ease off. One is the 'grave dignity' with which the sub-tale of the Oldest Animals is recounted, each animal stressing that it will help only because the inquirers are messengers of Arthur. Another is the errand of Menw son of Teirgwaedd, Arthur's shape-shifting magician, to establish that the treasures demanded by Ysbaddaden were actually present between the Twrch Trwyth's ears, *because it would be so mean to go to strive against him, if he did not have them,* showing a sense of responsibility rare in the tale. Even though the Twrch had been transformed by God into a boar because of his sins, the author seems at times to feel some pity for him, as well as awe and respect.

Opinions are also divided concerning Ysbaddaden himself. On the very last page, after his callous 'shaving' to the jawbone, he acknowledges defeat in a dignified speech:

Do not thank me for that, but Arthur who achieved it for you. Of my will you should never have won her. And now, my life – it is high time to take it.

Most of the opponents are dispatched swiftly and heartlessly, but Ysbaddaden seems to provide a more thoughtful note on which to end the tale.

With these characteristics in mind we can examine the portrayal of Arthur himself. As already remarked, we cannot expect to find depth of character; but we do find an energetic campaigner, very different from the sedentary lord of later romances. He is addressed by Culhwch, rhetorically currying favour before requesting Arthur's help, as *Penn Teyrned yr Ynys honn* ('chief of the lords of this island'): we might loosely compare this obscure title, which recurs in the Triads, with that of *dux bellorum* in the HISTORIA BRITTONUM. Arthur takes decisions by asking the opinions of his men, leading as first among equals, much as Robin Hood is imagined to have led his men; he selects his warriors and sends them on errands for which they are suited by their particular magical gifts; and he plays an active part in several of the quests, including the climactic boar hunt, leading from the front. He is not, however, described as a 'king', although he has a *llys* ('court') with established conventions. It is situated at an unknown place in Cornwall, *Kelli wic* ('the forest grove'). It is unlikely that the author had an actual place in mind; more probably, this was a literary phrase conveying the idea that Arthur and his men lived outside normal society, in the areas where ordinary men did not live, similar again to Robin Hood.

In keeping with this image, Arthur is not fitted into the normal historical pattern of rulers' pedigrees. He is consistently absent from the early Welsh genealogies, and is never given a patronym in the earliest Welsh texts; in lacking this attribute he stands in notable contrast with other heroes in the Welsh Triads. As far as our information goes, it was Geoffrey of Monmouth who first established Arthur's ancestry. CULHWCH provides Arthur with a number of kinsmen, including a son (Gwydre, slain in a passing moment by the Twrch), in-laws and maternal kin; one of the last, *Gormant mab Ricca*, was son of the *chief elder of Cornwall*, suggesting that Arthur's mother was of the Cornish aristocracy. But Arthur and his men lived outside the network of lords and paternal kindred which formed the basis of medieval Welsh society. This in turn contributes to what Sims-Williams has aptly described as *the wonderful, irresponsible atmosphere of an Arthurian past*. The number of Arthur's men who die so that Culhwch wins Olwen may achieve the comic effect of mismatch between the end and the means, but it also illustrates Arthur's lack of worries, even concerning his own men. The only moment when Arthur appears distressed by the ravages of the Twrch Trwyth occurs when the Twrch leaves south Wales and makes for Cornwall. The callousness with which enemies are dispatched, Arthur's unconcern with the normal governance of society and his lack of the normal ties of paternal kindred all contribute to this carefree, escapist atmosphere.

At one point Arthur enumerates his most important possessions, the exceptions to his offer to Culhwch of anything he might ask:

you shall receive the gift that your head and tongue specify, as far as wind dries, as rain wets, as sun reaches, as sea stretches and as earth exists – except for my ship, my cloak, Caledfwlch my sword, Rhongomyniad my spear, Wyneb Gwrthucher my shield, Carnwennan my knife, and Gwenhwyfar my wife.

The ordering of these possessions, with Gwen-hwyfar placed last as if an afterthought, is no doubt deliberately incongruous. All the names are readily meaningful to a Welsh audience: *Caledfwlch* ('Hard-notch'), *Rhongomyniad* ('Spear-striker'), *Wyneb Gwrthucher* ('Face-to-evening'), *Carnwennan* ('Whitehilted one'), and *Gwenhwyfar* ('White-phantom'). Arthur's ship is elsewhere named as *Prydwen* ('Fair-form') (in 'Preiddiau Annwn') and his cloak as *Gwenn* ('White') (in THE DREAM OF RHONABWY). The important aspect of the list is what the author considered to be Arthur's essential possessions: they mostly form a warrior's personal equipment. The ship was used in his adventures, both in CULHWCH and in the overseas expedition of 'Preiddiau Annwn'. We learn from a later text, the 'Thirteen Treasures of the Island of Britain', that Arthur's cloak made its wearer invisible. Arthur's hunting dog, Cafall, whom we have already met in the HISTORIA BRITTONUM, appears later in the story, in the hunt of the Twrch, and so does his hall, *Ehangwen* ('Broad-fair'). Arthur lived for his adventures, and his possessions were adapted to meet his literary needs.

One last question must be asked regarding this text: when the author of the HISTORIA BRITONNUM, in the ninth century, referred to Arthur's hunting of the Twrch Trwyth, was it already believed to have been performed in order to win Olwen as bride for Culhwch? There is no sure answer to this question. It is reasonable to wonder whether the great boar hunt was instead an Arthurian tale in its own right. Geoffrey of Monmouth referred to Arthur himself as *aper Cornubiae* ('the boar of Cornwall'), and Arthur's equivalent in Irish literature, Fionn, had a special interest in hunting, particularly wild boars. Perhaps the well-known hunt was appropriated by the author of CULHWCH in telling the story of 'Winning the giant's daughter', thus linking his folk tale to the Arthurian legend in order to render his telling of it the most elaborate and memorable one imaginable.

The poem 'Pa ŵr yw'r porthor?' has much in common with CULHWCH, in content and, partly, in mood. Like the prose tale, it uses the device of allusion to evoke a range of other Arthurian adventures. The plot is the rudimentary one of Arthur's explaining who he is to a gatekeeper in order to obtain admission, seemingly to his own court. Unfortunately the poem is incomplete, breaking off in mid-sentence owing to the loss of a page or pages in the manuscript; it is unknown how much is lost. Because of the situation, it is Arthur himself who here recalls his earlier adventures; his reminiscences become so extensive that, about halfway through, we begin to feel that Arthur (and the poet?) has forgotten the original question; in the surviving text we never return to the starting point, to resolve the situation portrayed there.

As in CULHWCH, the atmosphere is one of wonders and geographical expansiveness, with references to adventures set in Edinburgh and Anglesey, and perhaps Cornwall, though not outside Britain; the whole gives the impression of Arthur and his men as a group of adventurers roaming in search of excitement. There is enough common ground with CULHWCH for one almost to imagine the two works having the same author; but, although several adventures are mentioned in both texts, there are also several in the shorter poem which the author of CULHWCH failed to work into his wide-ranging story. There are a few minor inconsistencies between the two, though they are not such as would have worried someone with the enthusiasm shown by the author of CULHWCH. Assuming that the two works have different authors, the overlap of material is encouraging, since it suggests that CULHWCH, the more extensive text, really gives us a true overall impression of the kind of Arthurian material available to a Welsh author in about 1100. The poem begins with Arthur's question at the gate, but the porter quickly gains the dominant role:

> – *What man is the gatekeeper?*
> – *Glewlwyd Gafaelfawr:*
> *what man asks it?*
> – *Arthur, and fair Cai.*
> – *What attendance have you?*
> – *The best men in the world.*
> – *Into my house you shall not come,*
> *unless you vouch for them.*
> – *I shall vouch for them,*
> *and you shall see them:*
> *the vultures of Elái,*
> *all three of them wizards;*
> *Mabon son of Modron,*
> *servant of Uthr Pendragon;*
> *Cyscaint son of Banon,*
> *and Gwyn Goddyfrion.*
> *Brave were my men,*
> *defending their just claims . . .*

From this point on Arthur alone speaks, and the poem is composed in the past tense as he recalls, for a further seventy-one surviving lines, the former glories achieved by his men, with a particular emphasis on Cai's exploits, and the fearsome monsters encountered by all of them.

Several broad problems of interpretation arise. Glewlwyd appears elsewhere as Arthur's own gatekeeper on special occasions: on New Year's Day alone in CULHWCH; and at the *three chief festivals* of Easter, Whitsun and Christmas in GERAINT; in OWAIN

Arthur lacks a gatekeeper but Glewlwyd stands in. Glewlwyd is not known in another role in Welsh literature. Is Arthur, therefore, trying to gain admission to his own court in the poem? But Glewlwyd refers to 'my house'. We might anyway have expected Arthur and Glewlwyd to recognize each other, whatever the house. As with Culhwch's admission into Arthur's court in the prose tale, and the very similar scene in that tale when Cai arrives at the court of Wrnach the Giant, the author of the poem was playing upon the common theme of gaining access to a lord past his over-zealous porter. A similar scene appears in the brief story of St Germanus and his dramatic visit to Benlli in the ninth-century HISTORIA BRITTONUM. In setting such a scene, the author of 'Pa ŵr yw'r porthor?' need not even have had a specific story in mind, although it might be legitimate to suppose that he did.

The atmosphere is generally light-hearted, with rapid movement of ideas and allusions, and verbal play similar to that found in CULHWCH; but Arthur's reminiscences offer a nostalgic balance, creating a tone that is 'elegiac' (Sims-Williams) at times. The situation portrayed may be deliberately incongruous, for humorous effect, or there may be a more serious aspect. Sims-Williams has suggested that perhaps we see here an Arthur living beyond his era and down on his luck: there is a mention of a time *when Kelli was lost* which, if it refers to *Kelli wic* in Cornwall, may indeed suggest that Arthur is seeking admission to another's residence.

As in CULHWCH, we learn more about Arthur's world than about Arthur himself; what we learn is broadly consistent with the prose tale. Arthur and his men appear as if free of normal responsibilities, living for their adventures; their opponents are supernatural creatures – dog-headed monsters in Edinburgh, Palug's Cat (which would eat nine score warriors for its dinner) on Anglesey, a witch fought by Arthur, reminiscent of the one whom he bisected in CULHWCH, and a further nine witches transfixed by Cai. The battle of *traethev Trywruid* ('the shores of Tryfrwyd'), mentioned as the River *Tribruit* in the ninth-century List of Battles, was notable for the opponent fought in it, Garwlwyd ('Rough-grey'), known in the Triads as Gwrgi Garwlwyd. This is one of only two of the battles in that early list which are attributed to Arthur in a later source. Cai is also portrayed fighting along with Llachau, who is known in an *englyn* poem as Arthur's son (see p. 51), and who had an untimely end in battle, like Arthur's son Amr in the HISTORIA. But, as always, these characters and stories are swept tantalizingly past us; we never hear a full story. Along with other multiples of three (nine witches, nine score warriors), a reference to *nine hundred [men] listening, and six hundred being scattered* recalls, both in its poetic exaggeration and in its mathematics, the legendary 960 men whom Arthur killed in a single attack in the List of Battles.

Because of the incompleteness of the poem, it is difficult to assess the nature of Arthur's role in it. There are two reasons for considering it in part a light-hearted one: the situation of Arthur, the greatest leader of warriors, having to give an account of himself in order to gain admission to a hall, whether his own or another's, is inherently undignified; and the manner in which Arthur digresses into his reminiscences, losing the original track of the conversation, makes him appear somewhat awkward, even though harking back to former glories is also a serious, and recurrent, theme of later Arthurian literature. It is also a theme of Fenian literature in Irish, notably of the twelfth-century text ACALLAM NA SENÓRACH ('The Colloquy of the Ancients'). As for Arthur's role in the adventures mentioned, it is similar to that seen in CULHWCH, as far as can be judged. Arthur took an active part in several of the encounters; and his men, chiefly Cai and Bedwyr, had particular qualities, used in their own martial achievements. Arthur's reference to his men *defending their just claims* (*detvon*, 'deddfon') hints at the chivalric ethos of later romance, like the clearer hint provided by Arthur's statement in CULHWCH already quoted.

As a final comparison with 'Pa ŵr yw'r porthor?' a late medieval English ballad deserves a mention, for the partial similarity of situation which it offers. This is the fragmentary ballad known as 'King Arthur and King Cornwall', no. 30 in Francis Child's great collection. King Arthur was told by his queen, Guenever, that there was another king even more splendid than himself; he vowed not to rest until he had proved this to his own satisfaction. Eventually Arthur and his men arrived at the castle of King Cornwall:

> 'Come hither, thou proud porter,
>   I pray thee come hither to me . . .
>
> 'Tell who may be lord of this castle,' he sayes,
>   'Or who is lord in this cuntry?'
>
> 'Cornewall King,' the porter sayes,
>   'There is none soe rich as hee . . .'

> 'Pray him for one nights lodging and two meales meate,
>   For his love that dyed uppon a tree . . .'

> Then forth is gone this proud porter,
>   As fast as he cold hye,
> And when he came befor Cornewall King,
>   He kneeled downe on his knee.

> Sayes, 'I have beene porter-man, at thy gate,
>   This thirty winter and three . . .'

Arthur and his five companions stayed the night, and discovered that King Cornwall was not only wealthy but endowed with magical powers, and that he claimed to have fathered a daughter by Queen Guenever. He possessed a fearsome beast, the Burlow-beanie, which Arthur and his men tamed, and which then helped them to exploit King Cornwall's magical devices, to steal his sword and, finally, to cut off his head. The similarities with 'Pa ŵr yw'r porthor?' are not close; the story in the ballad is ultimately derived from, or at least akin to, a similar legend told of Charlemagne journeying to Constantinople to visit the emperor, for a similar purpose. That legend may be as old as the eleventh century, and it was known in later medieval Wales.

The story in the ballad of Arthur asking the porter for lodging, gaining admission, vanquishing the monster and killing the ruler of the court with his own sword would be thoroughly at home in an early Welsh Arthurian text. In the ballad, King Arthur asks the questions at the gate, though later King Cornwall, before boasting of his liaison with Guenever, prudently asks his guest whether he knows King Arthur: the dramatic irony of this non-recognition again bears comparison with the scene in 'Pa ŵr yw'r porthor?' The distant parallel provided by this ballad enables us to envisage a possible context for the scene in 'Pa ŵr yw'r porthor?', even though there is no means of knowing whether it is at all similar to that intended by the author of the Welsh poem.

Overall, these two texts, CULHWCH and 'Pa ŵr yw'r porthor?', constitute the fullest evidence for the atmosphere conjured up in a Welsh literary imagination by the name of Arthur. It is a world of magic and monsters, rapid-fire adventures and the outwitting or overpowering of supernatural opponents. It is a world far removed from the heroic one of the GODODDIN, from the emotive one of the *englyn* poetry (personal emotions, like characterization, play little part in early Arthurian literature), and from the moralistic caution of the Four Branches. The folk-tale world which Arthur and his men inhabit is in both cases seen through a light-hearted filter. Arthur appears as a leader, rather than a ruler: he leads his warriors without the responsibility of paternal ties of kindred, nor does he apparently suffer from the worries that afflict rulers such as Pwyll, Bendigeidfran or Urien Rheged. Although we shall find him described as 'king' in a few early texts, even before Geoffrey of Monmouth elevated him to imperial status, in these two works the nature of his leadership is much closer to that of Fionn in Irish literature, or Robin Hood in medieval English. Fionn's band of warriors was known in early Irish as a *fían* ('warriorband') and a dictionary definition of that word provides a perfect description of Arthur and his men as portrayed in our two texts: *a band of roving men whose principal occupations were hunting and war*. As seen in these texts, Arthur and his men constitute a

Welsh equivalent of an early Irish *fían*. The prose tale and the poem fill out the picture provided by the earlier HISTORIA BRITTONUM; but they do not necessarily show that the image of Arthur had changed between the ninth century and the early twelfth, as is often assumed: rather they provide the literary context of the character who had additionally become renowned as the defender of his island against its invaders, just as Fionn was in Ireland.

IV

Other Texts of the Central Middle Ages

A number of other texts from the central Middle Ages complement what is learnt from CULHWCH and 'Pa ŵr yw'r porthor?'. They all, for one reason or another, allude to Arthurian stories while primarily concentrating upon some other theme and, therefore, they expand Arthur's repertoire of adventures, though without significantly altering the overall picture of Arthur himself. The works examined in this section all date probably from the tenth to the twelfth century, though typically they cannot be dated much more closely than that, except for those by named poets in the twelfth century; many of these works cannot therefore be securely placed earlier or later than Geoffrey's crucial HISTORY, completed in about 1138.

The most important of these texts is the poem 'Preiddiau Annwn' ('The Spoils of Annwn'). This is one of the poems composed as if spoken by the legendary Taliesin, the embodiment of poetic inspiration who has been everywhere, been everything, experienced everything, and knows everything and who therefore speaks with an authority and a confidence which no rival can hope to match. Among his experiences is the adventure which forms the main theme of this poem, accompanying Arthur on a disastrous overseas expedition to Annwn, the fairy-world. As is usual in medieval Welsh, the poem does not narrate the story but merely alludes to it, for the purpose of enabling Taliesin to display once again his exceptional knowledge. The recurrent refrain, *Three ship-loads we went out; except for seven men, none returned*, emphasizes how privileged we are to be listening to one of the survivors.

The poem is of greater importance for the legend of Taliesin than for that of Arthur, in that it tells us more about Taliesin – his claims to different kinds of knowledge, his relationship with clerical scholars whose learning was more limited than his own, and his tribute to the Christian God as his (sole?) acknowledged lord – than its allusions tell us about the Arthurian adventure itself. Nevertheless, some important facts emerge, and it is a fair assumption that the poem refers to an existing legend about an overseas expedition by Arthur: there would be no apparent motive for Taliesin to make the story an Arthurian one if it were not so already.

The main purpose of the expedition was to free a prisoner, Gwair, held in the overseas stronghold. This aim may be compared with the freeing of two prisoners, Eiddoel fab Aer and Mabon son of Modron, in two separate episodes in CULHWCH (nominally to achieve two of the tasks set by the giant), and it again foreshadows the later chivalric code of Welsh and other romances, where aiding people in distress played so prominent a role. In his dialogue with the eagle, Arthur naïvely hopes to free Eliwlad, his dead nephew, from heaven (see p. 65). 'Preiddiau Annwn' informs us that Arthur demonstrated his *gwrhyt* ('manly courage') on the expedition. A secondary purpose was the acquisition of a magical cauldron, *kindled by the breath of nine maidens*, which would not cook food for a coward; this aim, too, recalls both CULHWCH, where one of the tasks was to acquire the cauldron of Diwrnach the Irishman, and the Second Branch of the Mabinogi. We are left to imagine what went so dreadfully wrong that only seven men returned, but the comparison with the Second Branch of the Mabinogi is so close that it may provide some idea. Bendigeidfran there invaded Ireland to rescue his sister Branwen; a magical cauldron helped the Irish in the ensuing battle; and Taliesin was one of the seven survivors. (Arthur is of course absent from this story, as from the whole of the Four Branches.) This parallel and others to 'Preiddiau Annwn' have been discussed by Sims-Williams, who justly suggests that attempting to connect the various stories in a genetic relationship would be misguided: the similarities are an instructive indication that, in considering medieval Welsh literature, we do better to think rather in terms of floating themes and plots, which could be attached to characters as an author might please.

The importance of 'Preiddiau Annwn' for the present study is that it extends Arthur's catalogue of adventures, and in a direction slightly different from that seen already: here we must suppose that his opponents were the fairy-folk, the inhabitants of Annwn; and that Arthur overreached himself, since the outcome was so disastrous, although (like Bendigeidfran's expedition to Ireland) it may have been a technical success if we assume that Gwair, one of the 'Three Exalted Prisoners' in a Triad along with Mabon, was indeed rescued. The fairy-folk are, of course, consistent with Arthur's other supernatural opponents, though of a slightly different order from monsters, witches and giants. The atmosphere of the poem is a solemn, majestic one, in contrast with that of CULHWCH and 'Pa ŵr yw'r porthor?' – primarily so in order to suit Taliesin's purpose of dealing in matters of cosmic significance. The earlier tale of Arthur killing his son Amr must also have been a tragic one, so the light-hearted atmosphere of our two chief texts need not be an accurate reflection of the early Welsh Arthurian corpus as a whole (see chapter IX).

The next group of texts provides a further extension to Arthur's repertoire. The Welsh-Latin Lives of saints appear late on the scene in European terms: the earliest surviving text was composed in about 1100, when writers in most European countries, including England, Ireland and Brittany, had been composing in the genre for several centuries. Arthur appears in several of the Welsh Lives, but he is absent from other important ones, including those of David, Beuno, Cybi and Teilo. Those incorporating the greatest amount of Arthurian material are the Lives of Cadog, Carannog and Gildas; and the Lives of Illtud and Padarn are also instructive.

Arthur's appearances in these works must be understood in the context of their purpose. The authors of the Lives were writing centuries after their subjects had lived and usually had no reliable information about them; they had to fall back on literary borrowings, local legends and their own imaginations to provide their material. The legendary character of the Lives is exemplified by the fact that several of them portray encounters between their heroes and Arthur. Their purpose was to glorify their saint and the monastery where he was honoured, if necessary at the expense of rival saints, secular rulers or other figures. One way of achieving this was to make the saint come into contact with secular lords, get the better of them, and be rewarded by land-grants or other privileges. (In an imaginative inversion of this convention, the author of CULHWCH made the saints of Ireland come to Arthur and ask for his protection when he landed in Ireland in pursuit of the Twrch Trwyth.) This role did not necessarily mean that the secular ruler was conceived in a negative light, any more than a rival saint outshone by the subject of the Life was so conceived. But another common theme was to portray the secular ruler as an evil pagan, hostile to the saint's work of conversion; in that case, he would be beaten by the saint, and either experience an unpleasant end or himself undergo conversion. Arthur does not play this latter role in the Welsh Lives.

It is agreed that the Lives with which we are concerned date from the twelfth century, several from around 1100–30, before the composition of Geoffrey of Monmouth's HISTORY; however, as with vernacular literature, the manuscripts are later, and the texts could in theory have received alterations after that date. Geoffrey gave Arthur dealings with various saints, notably *Dubricius* (Dyfrig), David, Samson and *Piramus* (the Cornish Piran?); but the following Arthurian episodes have little in common with Geoffrey's HISTORY and are assumed to be independent of it.

St Cadog was the patron saint of the abbey of Llancarfan, in Glamorgan, and his Life was written there by Lifris, who died in 1104. In the Life, Arthur appears in two separate contexts. He participates in a rather dubious episode in which the saint is conceived by means of King Gwynllyw's abduction of Gwladus, daughter of the saintly King Brychan of Brycheiniog. In an account reminiscent of CULHWCH, the abduction and King Brychan's angry pursuit are spotted by Arthur while he sits on a hilltop playing dice with his two companions, Cai and Bedwyr; they are described as *three valiant heroes*. In accordance with the atmosphere of the vernacular tale, Arthur's first reaction is to fancy the abducted girl for himself; but Cai and Bedwyr restrain him from such a crime (as they call it), reminding him *We are in the habit of helping those in need or distress*; so Arthur reluctantly adjudicates between the two kings. (Gwladus's own opinion is not considered.) As in CULHWCH, this passing remark of Cai and Bedwyr intriguingly foreshadows the chivalric code of the later romances. Because Gwynllyw has already crossed the border into his own territory, Arthur and his companions decide to support him, and fight back the army of the angry father. This enables Gwynllyw to proceed with his intention of marrying Gwladus, and thus St Cadog is born.

The episode is remarkable for its moral stance; later in the same Life it is acknowledged that St Cadog's father Gwynllyw had been of very loose morals, but at the urging of Cadog and Gwladus had mended his ways so as to lead a holy life. A slightly later Life of St Gwynllyw himself omits these problematical aspects of his character, and it is unclear why Lifris should have included them; the details which reflect so poorly upon Cadog's father seem unnecessary. But for our purpose the significant point is the portrayal of Arthur as a capricious character. This is in contrast with his statement in CULHWCH which seems to prefigure the chivalric code (*The greater the bounty we may give, the greater our nobility, fame and honour;*

see p. 21), though it accords with the generally irresponsible atmosphere of Arthur's world in that tale.

The other Arthurian episode in St Cadog's Life is similar. The saint is required to arbitrate in Arthur's attempts to enforce vengeance upon a local leader who had killed three of Arthur's warriors; Cadog decrees that Arthur should receive cattle in compensation. Arthur unhelpfully demands cattle of a magical colour (red in front and white behind), which St Cadog obligingly creates out of ordinary cattle. These are handed over to Arthur, Cai and Bedwyr at a ford, but they turn into bracken as soon as Arthur takes possession of them. This makes the leader realize the error of his ways, and he grants to St Cadog the privilege of sheltering fugitives in sanctuary at his monastery. In order to strengthen the force of this grant, Arthur is here termed a king (*rex*), probably the earliest occasion, in any language, that such a term is found applied to him. A very similar episode is told in the Irish-Latin Life of St Ciarán of Saighir (undated, but known from a fourteenth-century manuscript): the hero's namesake, St Ciarán of Clonmacnoise, is imprisoned by a king, who will release him only for a ransom of seven red cows with white heads; these St Ciarán of Saighir produces. After being paid over they vanish again, and the king repents of his sin.

Arthur's grant of sanctuary-rights to St Cadog was later confirmed, according to Lifris, by the north-Welsh king Maelgwn and his son Rhun. The story told here was evidently known in local legend, for the writer cites two place-names, *Tref redinauc* (Tredunnock, 'brackeny farm'), and *Rith guurtebou*

40

('the ford of the rejoinders'), which show where the events occurred and demonstrate the truth of the story. The main point of relating the saint's encounter with Arthur was to demonstrate the authority of the privileges enjoyed by the monastery, and Arthur was evidently a suitable figure to impart that authority.

It is notable that Arthur's own religious stance is not an issue in these episodes. They are not examples of a pagan king opposing the saint's work of conversion, for Arthur is neutral on that crucial matter; he merely wishes to achieve his own particular aims. In contrast, therefore, with other stereotyped rulers in this genre of literature, he appears as headstrong and capricious, but not hostile to the saints or to Christianity in general. His two favoured companions, Cai and Bedwyr, are those seen in 'Pa ŵr yw'r porthor?'; Arthur's description as a 'hero' or 'champion' is in keeping with what we have seen so far, and his concerns are the carefree ones of CULHWCH. Vengeance for his dead warriors was of course a serious concern of a leader; but the manner in which Arthur follows it up suggests personal pique as much as responsible lordship. We tend today to think of saints' Lives as a serious genre of literature; but there is no reason why particular episodes should not have had a light-hearted tone, provided they served the overall purpose of the work.

Other saints' Lives are consistent with this picture. St Carannog was the patron saint of Llangrannog in Ceredigion, and his brief First Life was written probably for that church in the twelfth century. Arthur is portrayed in it as a king (*rex*), ruling not in

Wales but in south-west England (Somerset and Cornwall), jointly with another ruler, Cadwy (*Cato*). The saint arrives in Somerset, having followed his floating altar across the Bristol Channel. Arthur *joyfully received a blessing* from St Carannog – again he is not hostile to Christianity. Carannog asks if Arthur knows where his altar is, and Arthur promises to tell him in return for a favour from the saint, namely ridding the district of a troublesome dragon. Carannog tames it easily, and Arthur returns his altar to him, having unsuccessfully tried to use it as a table. (This is the earliest known reference to such an item of household furniture in relation to Arthur; but of course an altar would not have been circular, so it is not a reference to the Round Table.) Arthur gives the saint a written charter of land in Somerset in perpetuity, and additional land further west, presumably at the parish of Crantock in Cornwall. This was the main purpose of the encounter from the writer's point of view, since it enhanced the Welsh saint's prestige to own land across the water; again it necessitated portraying Arthur as a landowning ruler. But the taming of the dragon was also important: it is of a type with the Arthurian encounters with monsters that we have already examined, but here St Carannog is seen to be even better than the king himself at this Arthurian speciality. The saint's prestige was enhanced, at the minor expense of the secular hero. The idea of Arthur having in his territory a dragon which he and his warriors could not themselves overcome may have been a light-hearted, incongruous detail. Arthur's capriciousness again comes across, as in the Life of St Cadog, through his bargaining stance towards the saint: I'll tell you where your altar is, if you'll do me a favour.

42

The Life of St Illtud was probably written for that saint's monastery of Llanilltud Fawr (Llantwit Major, Glamorgan), in the mid-twelfth century. The saint is portrayed as having been a successful secular lord in his early life, who was converted to lead the holy life of a monk. In his secular career he was honourably received and given gifts at the court of his kinsman King (*rex*) Arthur; the location of the court is unfortunately not stated. Here again Arthur is neutral in terms of his religious allegiance; his role is to demonstrate the high secular standing which the saintly hero renounced in favour of the religious life. St David was similarly given a claimed relationship with Arthur, though that is found earliest in Geoffrey's HISTORY and could have been created by him.

St Padarn was the patron saint of Llanbadarn Fawr, near Aberystwyth, and his Life was presumably composed for that church, perhaps in about 1120–30. There is a brief Arthurian episode which is consistent with those already seen: King Arthur, visiting the saint, takes a fancy to his tunic, and desires it for himself. Padarn understandably refuses to give it to him, and Arthur attempts to take it by force. But, at the saint's prayer, the ground opens up and engulfs Arthur up to the neck; Arthur asks forgiveness of the saint, and adopts Padarn as his eternal patron. Once again Arthur's childlike capriciousness is the key to the episode; curiously no benefits granted by him to the saint are mentioned, though they may be implied by his adoption of Padarn as his patron.

Finally, the Life of St Gildas by Caradog of Llancarfan, probably of similar early twelfth-century date, contains two Arthurian episodes. The first is unlocated; it concerns Gildas's twenty-three brothers, who consistently oppose Arthur, the king (*rex*) of all Britain, whereas Gildas himself is loving towards him. The eldest brother, Huail, is especially resistant, and often wages war against Arthur from Scotland, for he will not acknowledge any king. (The same statement is made of him in CULHWCH – as a warrior at Arthur's court!) During one such raid he is killed by King Arthur. Gildas is in Ireland at the time, and prays both for his brother's soul and for King Arthur's, thereby showing his own strength of forgiveness, which in turn induces (we are told) King Arthur's repentance, penance and amended way of life. Gerald of Wales, in the 1190s, added the detail that Gildas threw into the sea all that he had written in praise of Arthur – the earliest attempt to explain Gildas's silence concerning the hero. Once again Arthur's religious allegiance does not arise. If this Life is earlier than Geoffrey of Monmouth's HISTORY OF THE KINGS OF BRITAIN, then it is the earliest source to make Arthur 'King of all Britain'. The episode is of interest particularly because it had a long life in local legend: a stone in the town of Ruthin (Denbighshire) is still known as the place where Arthur beheaded Huail (see p. 104).

The second episode is set in Somerset, where St Gildas is asked to adjudicate between a King Melwas (*Meluas rex*), ruling there, and Arthur, described as a king (*tyrannus*) whose wife Guinevere (*Guennuuar*) has been abducted by Melwas. Arthur, having searched for Guinevere and her abductor for a year, eventually finds them in Glastonbury and besieges them there, with an army drawn from Cornwall and Devon. The abbot of Glastonbury, accompanied by Gildas, intervenes and advises

Melwas to relinquish his captive. (Once again Guinevere's opinion is left tantalizingly unclear.) The two kings, in gratitude for his peacemaking, both give extensive lands to the abbot. The episode serves little apparent purpose, except for giving St Gildas a link with Glastonbury. Although Arthur is described as a *tyrannus*, that need not have had the opprobrious connotation that 'tyrant' does today; perhaps it meant a petty or lesser king compared with a *rex*. (Melwas, unlike Arthur, receives the adjective *iniquus*, 'unjust'.) Glastonbury Abbey had one or two links with Cornwall in the Middle Ages, and it is possible that Arthur's role here as donor was to explain those links, while Melwas's contribution to the abbey's property would have been envisaged as lands in Somerset.

There is every reason to think that this is an older story which was used by Caradog. The saint himself has virtually no role in it, but merely accompanies the abbot on his pacific mission; and, unlike the abbot, Gildas gains nothing from the episode, except for the prestige of being associated with the two kings and involved in a (presumably) well-known event. There are later references to Melwas's abduction of Guinevere; it is possible that the legend provided inspiration both for Geoffrey of Monmouth's story of how Modred, Arthur's nephew, abducted Guinevere and usurped the crown of Britain while Arthur was campaigning abroad, and also, more surely, for Chrétien's story of Guinevere's abduction by Meleagant in his romance of Lancelot. We shall return to the legend later (see pp. 67–9); the importance of this episode lies more in Guinevere's abduction than in Arthur's own role. As before, he imparts reflected glory to the saint (once again at no detriment to himself), though in this case it is of a very indirect nature, and the story seems to serve the interests of Glastonbury Abbey rather than St Gildas. It is worth noting also that, unusually, there is nothing supernatural in this episode as it stands: if a distinction were to be made, the Arthur portrayed here would be Arthur the soldier, rather than the Arthur of the Wonders of Britain.

Overall, the image of Arthur provided by these Lives is similar to that in the Welsh-language texts: he is a leader of men – a landed ruler, when it suits the needs of the story – accompanied by Cai and Bedwyr (in the Life of St Cadog), the hero of local legends, living in a fairy-tale world of magical animals (the cattle and the dragon, standard fare in saints' Lives) and of legendary or semi-legendary kings (Gwynllyw, Brychan, Maelgwn, Rhun, Melwas: how Arthur's kingdom, if he had one, related to theirs is not clear); he is subject to passing whims and fancies, but is not ill-disposed to the saints, nor hostile in principle to Christianity. Henken has justly summed up his character as *spoiled, demanding what he fancies, but basically well-meaning*, contrasting his role with that of the more malevolent King Maelgwn of Gwynedd.

Although these Lives provide the earliest evidence for Arthur as a 'king', they are consistently vague about his geographical domain: he appears wherever his presence is required for the action of the story, whether in south-east Wales (as in CULHWCH, and where several of the Lives were composed and concentrated their action), mid-Wales (in St Padarn's Life) or in south-west England (in the Lives of both St Carannog and St Gildas, and of course in CULHWCH again). It is clear that the location of the earliest Arthurian stories in the Welsh Marches – indeed, in Wales at all – indicates not the priority of that region in the Arthurian legend, but merely where the author of the HISTORIA BRITTONUM obtained his material. On present evidence, no region can claim priority for the Arthurian legend, and it is possible that Arthur's status as 'king' was a literary invention, to suit the requirements of the Lives.

The remaining texts to be discussed in this section are from the Welsh poetry of the period, and are ones which emphasize the other side of Arthur seen in the HISTORIA BRITTONUM (if it is really a separate side), namely Arthur the soldier rather than the hero of supernatural legends. The first three poems are in the early *englyn* metre (three-line stanzas), which was used for various topics (religion, nature, saga material) from about the ninth century to the twelfth. The first is an elegiac lament for a leader called Geraint – possibly the real Cornish king of that name who lived in the early eighth century, though if so he has here become a figure of Welsh legend, and has been made a contemporary of the legendary Arthur; the author of CULHWCH did the same, making Geraint ab Erbin a warrior of Arthur's court. The association of the two figures has no significance for actual chronology, of course. The poem is not narrative but describes a battle in which Geraint took part, at an unidentified Llongborth (possibly Langport, in Somerset); it is not even clear who won the battle, or that Geraint is dead, although that is implied by the tone. Arthur, or at least Arthur's men, also took part in the battle, presumably on the same side.

Pan anet Gereint, oed agoret pyrth Nef;
. . .
gelyn y Seis, car y seint.
. . .

Yn Llongborth llas y Arthur
gwyr dewr: kymynynt a dur.
Amherawdyr, llywyawdyr llauur.

(When Geraint was born, the gates of Heaven were open;
. . .
an enemy to the Englishman, a friend to the saints.
. . .

In Longborth were killed, to Arthur's loss,
brave men: they struck down with steel.
The emperor, the leader in strife.)

The poem is of interest in connection with the later romance about Geraint, since a later section dwells on the horses which took part in the battle, describing them cumulatively for verbal effect; in his romance Geraint gathers a collection of horses from people whom he has beaten in his wanderings, and it is tempting to associate the two. The poem does not add greatly to our knowledge of Arthur; but his presence in the semi-heroic context of an elegy for a legendary warrior forms a useful balance to the monsters of CULHWCH and 'Pa ŵr yw'r porthor?' His description as an 'emperor' is curious: this word is unlikely to have been used of him before Geoffrey's HISTORY became well known in the mid-twelfth century. As Rowland has pointed out, this line would be at home in the Gogynfeirdd poetry of the twelfth and thirteenth centuries.

The next poem is from the same class of poetry as

GERAINT, namely the *englyn* poetry in which heroic stories and ideas are examined, questioned or brooded upon in an elegiac, contemplative, often wistful manner, well distanced from the direct approach of true heroic poetry in Welsh. ENGLYNION Y BEDDAU ('The Stanzas of the Graves'), in the thirteenth-century Black Book of Carmarthen, is a nostalgic evocation of landmarks around Wales which were believed to be the graves of heroes from a former age.

> Bet mab Ossvran yg Camlan,
> gvydi llauer kywlauan;
> bet Bedwir in alld Tryvan.
>
> (The grave of Ossvran's son at Camlan,
> after many an assault;
> the grave of Bedwyr on the slope of Tryfan.)

Most of the graves cannot be located, and often the heroes are unknown, though some known characters appear, such as Pryderi and Dylan from the Four Branches, Bedwyr and the later Arthurian heroes Owain ab Urien and Gwalchmai, Cynon fab Clydno from the GODODDIN, and Rhydderch Hael from the Myrddin legend. In this learned guide to Welsh antiquities, heroes from normally distinct literary categories appear side by side.

> Bet y March, bet y Guythyr,
> bet y Gugaun Cletyfrut;
> anoeth bid, bet y Arthur.
>
> (A grave for March, a grave for Gwythyr,
> a grave for Gwgawn Red-sword;
> the world's wonder, a grave for Arthur.)

'March' may be March ap Meirchion, the legendary king, uncle of Trystan and husband of Esyllt. As it happens, Gwythyr fab Greidyawl and Gwgawn Gleddyfrudd are both mentioned elsewhere in Arthurian contexts, Gwythyr among the many heroes mentioned in CULHWCH, and Gwgawn as a follower of Owain in the late tale BREUDDWYD RHONABWY (see chapter VII). The meaning of the last line has been much discussed; it is probably, 'Nobody can say where Arthur's grave is'. The word *anoeth* ('a wonder, a marvel'), is the same as that used in CULHWCH by Arthur and his men to refer to the treasures demanded by Ysbaddaden; but there need be no intended echo.

It is tempting, and reasonable, to see the line as a reference to the belief that Arthur was not dead but would come again. This idea first appears in the earlier twelfth century in external writings about the Welsh, Cornish and Bretons, including (in a typically cryptic allusion) Geoffrey of Monmouth's HISTORY OF THE KINGS OF BRITAIN. Most notably William of Malmesbury, in the 1120s, described Gawain's (Gwalchmai's) grave, fourteen feet long, on the seashore, but said *Arturis sepulcrum nusquam visitur* ('Arthur's grave is nowhere to be seen'). The remark, from an English observer who was not particularly sympathetic to the Arthurian legend, agrees well with this interpretation of the line in ENGLYNION Y BEDDAU; the line itself would then be the earliest allusion within Welsh itself to the belief that Arthur was not dead (it is not found again until much later, perhaps not until the sixteenth century), and so probably also, by implication, the earliest Welsh reference to his future return.

Arthur is named in a third *englyn* poem, 'The

Conversation of Gwyddnau Garanhir and Gwyn ap Nudd'. Gwyn ap Nudd is mentioned in CULHWCH in several contexts: God had put *the nature of the devils of Annwn into him, to prevent the world's ruin*, a service from which he could not be spared to take part in the boar hunt; and he was destined to fight with Gwythyr fab Greidyawl every May Day until the world's end, competing for Creiddylad, daughter of Lludd Silver-Hand. In this obscure poem Gwyn alludes, Taliesin-like, to famous warriors whose deaths he witnessed. One of these was Llachau, son of Arthur:

> *Mi a wum lle llas Llachev*
> *mab Arthur, uthir ig kertev,*
> *ban ryreint brein ar crev.*

> *(I was present where Llachau was killed,*
> *son of Arthur, awesome in songs,*
> *when ravens kept croaking over gore.)*

It is unclear whether the epithet 'awesome in songs' refers to Llachau or his father; probably Llachau, since he is the focus of the stanza, and also because he is consistently mentioned as a paragon of a warrior in the court poetry. The juxtaposition of Arthur's name with the adjective *uthr* ('awesome, terrifying') is striking in view of Geoffrey's naming of Uther Pendragon as Arthur's father; but it need have no special significance. We learn from this stanza both that Llachau was Arthur's son (so named also in the Triads) and that he died a warrior's death in battle.

The last poetry to be examined from the central Middle Ages is that of the twelfth-century members of the Gogynfeirdd, the court poets of the Welsh princes in the last two centuries of Welsh independence. These poets were concerned with praise for their patrons, or with religious topics; but they used earlier legends as comparisons for the martial or other qualities of their closer subjects, so once again we find them alluding to stories, including Arthurian legends, without narrating them. Naturally, since warlike virtues were one of their primary standards of excellence, when Arthur is mentioned it is usually as a paragon of valour in battle, as earlier in the GODODDIN; the supernatural side of Arthur's world is not detectable, although the poets and their audiences would doubtless have had both in mind. The references are of interest for what they tell us about the appreciation of the Arthurian legend by the poets of the period and their audiences.

Arthur himself was named by four poets in the twelfth century as a leader of men and as a standard of military valour and generosity. In the mid-twelfth century Gwalchmai ap Meilyr (was this poet named after Arthur's nephew?) praised Madog ap Maredudd, king of Powys (died 1160) for having *Arthur gedernyd* ('Arthur's strength'), and Cynddelw likened the sound of the same Madog's army to that of Arthur's band of warriors – *mal gawr torf teulu Arthur* ('like the clamour of the host of Arthur's warband'); Seisyll Bryffwrch, in his elegy for Owain ap Gruffudd, king of Gwynedd (died 1170), attributed *lluch ryfig Arthur* ('the lightning confidence of Arthur') to his subject.

The majority of the references to Arthur at this period occur in the works of Llywarch ap Llywelyn (Prydydd y Moch), who flourished *c.* 1170–1220, and for whom Arthur was a favoured comparison. Llywarch cited him as a paragon of strength, valour and generosity in his praise of various lords. In his elegy for Gruffudd ap Cynan ab Owain of Gwynedd (who died in 1200), he made reference to the triad of the 'Three Generous Men':

> Hael Arthur, modur myd angut, am rot,
> hael Ryderch am eurwut,
> hael Mordaf, hael mawrdec Nut,
> haelach, gretuolach, Gruffut.

> (Generous was Arthur, the battle-famous lord, in giving;
> generous was Rhydderch for golden bounty;
> generous was Mordaf, generous was great fair Nudd:
> more generous, more powerful, was Gruffudd!)

In the Triad itself Nudd, Mordaf and Rhydderch are named as the three, and then, in what looks like a later addition, *And Arthur himself was more generous than the three*. Prydydd y Moch's citation shows that he knew this Triad in the extended form in which we have it, including the intrusive Arthur.

One of Llywarch's references to Arthur is of a different kind; it comes in a poem to God, also attributed to Cynddelw. The poet, wishing to emphasize the transience of earthly glory, mentioned Arthur along with Alexander and Julius Caesar as empire-builders, and with Hercules and Bendigeidfran fab Llŷr as mythological heroes, all of whose days had passed.

> Rybu erthyst yn: rybu Arthur gynt;
> rybu amgyfrawd gwynt, gwan tra messur.
> Rybu Ull Kessar; keissyassei Fflur
> y gan ut Prydein, prid y hesgur.

(We have received a lesson: Arthur existed, once;
he was a whirlwind, attacking beyond measure.
Julius Caesar existed; he had sought Flora
from the lord of Britain – dearly he claimed her.)

Although critical of Arthur, this allusion does not de-
nigrate him – quite the reverse: he is named first in a
very distinguished company. The point is rather that
even these heroes could not conquer death and had
finally to face their maker. The context makes Arthur
an empire-builder, like Julius Caesar and Alexander;
this in turn suggests that the poet was aware of the
new dimension which the Arthurian legend had
received from Geoffrey of Monmouth's HISTORY OF
THE KINGS OF BRITAIN earlier in the twelfth century
(see chapter VI). Although the porter in CULHWCH
had attributed adventures on several continents to
Arthur, it was probably Geoffrey who first gave
Arthur imperial successes abroad, involving conquests comparable with those of Caesar or Alexander. (Compare Arthur's epithet *amherawdyr*
('emperor') in the *englyn* poem on Geraint, above.)
That Llywarch was aware of Geoffrey's work is
borne out by his use three times (in two poems, one
of them again attributed alternatively to Cynddelw)
of the term *Pendragon* to mean 'leader, ruler': the use
of this term again suggests the growing influence of
Geoffrey's HISTORY towards the end of the twelfth
century.

There are several unexpected features of the Arthurian allusions in the twelfth-century court poetry. One
is their small number: Arthur himself is named
seven times in the poetry down to 1200, but hardly
any of his warriors receives more than a single
mention. The exceptions are Medrawd, who causes

further surprise by the favourable nature of his references (see pp. 113–15); Arthur's son Llachau, of whom little is known, but who is mentioned four times by Cynddelw; and an even less well-known Arthurian character, Elifri, named by two twelfth-century poets. No Arthurian warrior receives as many mentions as Benlli Gawr (Benlli the Giant, burnt in his fortress by St Germanus in the HISTORIA BRITTONUM) or Ogrfan Gawr, another heroic giant. Both of these giants were tangentially Arthurian, in that Benlli was linked with Arthur by the thirteenth-century poet Bleddyn Fardd, and Ogrfan was said to be Gwenhwyfar's father; but the allusions suggest that they were named at this period as heroes in their own right.

A further unexpected feature is that most of the Arthurian references are found in the work of only two poets, Cynddelw and Prydydd y Moch, admittedly those with the largest corpus of surviving poetry. No other Gogynfardd poet in the twelfth century has more than a single Arthurian reference in his extant works, and several poets have none.

Llachau is also named in 'Pa ŵr yw'r porthor?', where Arthur alludes to his fighting along with Cai; and in the *englyn* poem concerning Gwyn ap Nudd, already examined. But little is known of him, and his absence from the long list of warriors named in CULHWCH has been noted earlier (p. 17). Cynddelw referred, in four different poems, to *Llacheu uar* ('Llachau's ferocity'); to one being as swift as Llachau (*Llacheu gyfred*); to Llachau's generosity, *llary Llacheu heuelys* ('generous on Llachau's scale'); and to the Lord Rhys (died 1197) as *Llacheu gyfarpar* ('of

Llachau's purposefulness'). It is likely that Cynddelw's fondness for him as a standard of comparison was partly due to the convenience of his name for purposes of consonance. His name is twice alliterated with *llachar* ('bright, dazzling'); and the later Gogynfeirdd showed a similar liking for his name. His popularity in this poetry serves to endorse his epithet in the earlier *englyn* poem, *uthir ig kertev* ('awesome in songs'), but it is still unclear whether he was actually as popular in storytelling as his mentions by the court poets would suggest.

Elifri is another of Arthur's warriors who receives a number of mentions, in the twelfth century by both Cynddelw, *alafrot Elifry* ('wealth-giving like Elifri', the Lord Rhys again) and Prydydd y Moch, *detyf Elifri* ('with Elifri's manner'), and by three others in the thirteenth century. Apart from these poetic allusions, he is known only in the romance of GERAINT, where he is named twice, once as Arthur's *penn maccwyf* ('chief esquire', perhaps his master of horses), and once with the epithet *Anaw Kyrd* ('wealth of skills'). Elifri's poetic reputation, like that of Llachau, seems out of proportion with what we know of him elsewhere. Since his name always occurs in rhyming position, it may again be that his popularity with the poets owed something to the form of his name; either that, or perhaps he was formerly more prominent in the Arthurian legend.

Other Arthurian allusions can be briefly mentioned: all the remaining twelfth-century ones, except for one, occur in the work of Cynddelw. The exception is a reference in a love poem by Hywel ab Owain, the poet-prince (died 1170), to his having been vexed and rejected in *llys Ogyruann* ('Ogrfan's court').

Other references to Ogrfan envisage him as a warlike hero, but it seems likely that this refers to Ogrfan as father of Gwenhywfar, and that Hywel was comparing himself with Arthur as a suitor for Gwenhwyfar; his reference to the lady as *Gwenn* ('the fair one') perhaps offers a further allusion to her name. (Since Ogrfan was a giant, we may be meant to think of Culhwch's suit for Olwen as well.) The reference, if present, is an indirect one, and the only one to Gwenhwyfar in the whole corpus of Gogynfeirdd poetry.

Cynddelw provides references, once more in passing, to Gwalchmai (Gawain), Dillus, Cai and *Kelli wic* in one poem, and to Twrch Trwyth and Camlan in another. In his long elegy for Owain of Gwynedd (died 1170, father of Hywel the poet-prince), Cynddelw likened Owain's court to *Kelli wic*, and Owain himself to Gwalchmai, *taerualch ual Gwalchmei* ('fervently-strong like Gwalchmai' – seemingly no allusion to Gwalchmai's golden-tongued peace-making), and also, in a single couplet, to both Dillus the bearded giant and Cai himself:

> *Grym dillut Dullus uab Eurei,*
> *gretyf Greidwyr a Chynyr a Chei.*

> *(With the irresistible power of Dillus son of Efrai,*
> *with the strength of Greidwyr, of Cynyr, and of Cai.)*

Greidwyr is unknown elsewhere, and Cynyr is Cai's father; although Cynddelw did not spell out a connection between Dillus and Cai, his mention of them in successive lines, both for their strength, naturally evokes the story in Culhwch whereby Cai and Bedwyr killed Dillus the Bearded. Cynddelw even made use of the same rhyme as Arthur did in his mocking *englyn* which so offended Cai, rhyming Cai's name with that of Dillus's father Efrai (or Eurai). These references do not tell us anything new about the literary heroes themselves; but Cynddelw could evidently assume that the audience of this poem would know of this episode in CULHWCH, and of Arthur's court at *Kelli wic*.

Cynddelw's long poem celebrating Owain's son Hywel, the poet-prince himself, contains several Arthurian references. It was here that he compared Hywel with Llachau in generosity; later in the same poem, in a sequence of images demonstrating Hywel's largesse, he made a more unexpected comparison.

> *Keffitor ymdwr am Drwyd heuelyt,*
> *Twrch teryt y ar uwyd.*
> *Caffawd beirt eu but yn yt wyd . . .*

> *(A throng is found around Trwyd's equal,*
> *a fervent Twrch over (his) food.*
> *Poets receive their bounty where you are . . .)*

There is slight obscurity, or play on words, here; but Cynddelw was clearly comparing Hywel ab Owain with the Twrch Trwyth. As in Germanic poetry, the image of a wild boar was often used as a simile for a warlike hero; so were those of the lion, wolf or eagle. Cynddelw's comparison is presumably based on the story known in CULHWCH, and it envisages the Twrch's ferocity, destructiveness and invincibility as martial virtues; the animal's opposition to Arthur was apparently not a drawback to the comparison. (We may recall Arthur's own sympathy for the

Twrch in CULHWCH, noted earlier.) The forms of the words are themselves of interest. Cynddelw's form *Trwyd* (the final *-d* proved by the rhymes in the passage) is at variance with *Trwyth*, the form given in our text of CULHWCH; but *Trwyd* was also used by other poets down to the fifteenth century, and it agrees with the form *Troit* in the HISTORIA BRITTONUM. *Trwyd* is, furthermore, the expected Welsh reflex of the equivalent Irish form of the name, *Tríath*, found in texts going back probably to the ninth century (compare Irish *líath*, Welsh *llwyd*, 'grey'). Evidently the form used by Cynddelw and later poets, *Trwyd*, was more 'correct' than that which our text of CULHWCH has transmitted. Other texts of the HISTORIA have the form *Terit*, 'Teryd', instead of *Troit*; this is suspiciously similar to Cynddelw's *Twrch teryt* ('a fervent (*terydd*) Twrch'), but that may be coincidental.

Later still in the same poem Cynddelw praised Hywel's success against enemies:

> *Gnawd gosgo gosgort yn diflan,*
> *Ual ymosgryn mawr Gawr Gamlan.*
>
> *(The host is sure to be bowed, fading away,*
> *as in the great contention of the Battle of Camlan.)*

Although it is not certain, the nature of the comparison seems almost to suggest that Camlan was seen as a successful battle, or at least not as the disaster which it had become in Geoffrey of Monmouth's HISTORIA. One or two later poetic mentions appear to carry a similar hint, namely that it was an event where honour was gained rather than one where a period of glory came to an end. The literary attitude to Camlan will have depended, of course, upon the attitude to Arthur himself and to Medrawd, and these are both potentially ambiguous (see chapters VIII and IX). Overall, the number of Arthurian references in this poem, and the abstruseness of those connected with Twrch Trwyth, may have formed an indirect compliment to Hywel's own literary expertise.

From the references in these two poems it is clear that Cynddelw, in around 1170, could allude to Arthurian stories and heroes, including those incorporated in CULHWCH, and to others now lost to us, and that they would be recognized and appreciated by his audience and patrons.

The Arthurian references found in the work of the twelfth-century Gogynfeirdd thus show us the legend occupying a place, though hardly a major one, in the body of legends upon which the poets might draw for their comparisons. They knew the stories that we know, notably those mentioned in CULHWCH and also the battle of Camlan, for which we are largely dependent upon the dubious authority of Geoffrey of Monmouth, and apparently further stories in which heroes absent from CULHWCH played roles, especially Elifri and Arthur's son Llachau. Medrawd was not the byword for treachery that he later became, and (if Hywel ab Owain's allusion is correctly interpreted) there may have been a story of Arthur's difficult suit for Gwenhwyfar from her father Ogrfan, perhaps comparable with Culhwch's suit for Olwen. It is instructive to find that the Arthurian legend was not as prominent in the work of these poets as it later became; perhaps the greater number of allusions seen in the work of Prydydd y

Moch, towards the end of the century, is a symptom of Arthur's growing international fame, resulting from the popularity of Geoffrey of Monmouth's HISTORY.

Finally in the twelfth century, Arthur is mentioned in the ITINERARIUM KAMBRIAE (*The Journey through Wales*) written in Latin by Gerald the Welshman in about 1190. Gerald recorded that a mountain, usually taken to be Pen-y-Fan, the highest of the Brecon Beacons, was known as *Kaerarthur*, which he translated as 'Arthur's seat' (his name is presumably an error for *Kadair Arthur*), because of its two peaks in the form of a chair. This name has an earlier parallel in Devon or Cornwall, where a rock called 'Arthur's chair' existed in about 1113, and a later one in the well-known hill in Edinburgh. Arthur's propensity for possessing pieces of household furniture around the countryside is a trait which will be discussed later (see pp. 102–6); for now the interest is that the name given by Gerald demonstrates the continuing interest in Arthur in local folklore of the late twelfth century, alongside the literary references which we have been examining, and similar to that recorded in the HISTORIA BRITTONUM, 360 years earlier.

Before leaving the central Middle Ages, it is important to note one body of material where Arthur is conspicuous by his absence: the prophetic poetry. Poems of this period, notably the tenth-century 'Armes Prydein' ('The Prophecy of Britain') and the prophetic poetry (twelfth-century?) attributed to Myrddin (Merlin), made mention of leaders whose return was eagerly awaited, who were to lead the Welsh to victory against the English and expel the intruders from Britain. The leaders named in these poems were consistently Cynan and Cadwaladr; Arthur never appears. Similarly in the prophetic 'Cyfoesi' ('Conversation') of Myrddin with Gwenddydd his sister (thirteenth-century?), in which Myrddin foretells the 'future' rulers of Wales and Britain, Arthur's notable absence shows that he was not considered to be a legendary king in the way that more historical figures such as Urien of Rheged and Maelgwn of Gwynedd (both named in the 'Cyfoesi') were seen. Even when Arthur was given kingly status, notably in the saints' Lives, he must have been imagined differently from characters such as these. Arthur's absence from the list of rulers in the 'Cyfoesi' is particularly striking in the context of Geoffrey of Monmouth's earlier glorification of him: either he was deliberately omitted from the list, or Geoffrey's influence had not yet penetrated this aspect of Welsh literary culture at the time when the poem was composed.

Arthur's absence from the prophetic poetry continued in later centuries. In due course, Owain Lawgoch (died 1378) and Owain Glyndŵr were added to Cynan and Cadwaladr as the awaited leaders, but still not Arthur. His absence from such a role in the poetry is all the more remarkable since there is good evidence from sources outside Wales that Arthur's return was eagerly anticipated – indeed, that is assumed to be one reason for the 'discovery' of his tomb at Glastonbury in about 1190, so as to dispel that hope. Similarly, Arthur was cast in the folk-tale role of the hero sleeping inside a hill, who would awaken in the hour of need. The earliest reference to this legend comes, strangely enough, from Sicily, where Gervase of Tilbury, in about 1211, recorded that Arthur had been seen, recovering from

Modred's wounds, in a palace on Mount Etna. The legend of Arthur is considered to have been taken to Sicily by the Normans, but it is surprising to find this particular aspect of it flourishing at that date. In the sixteenth century, a Welsh prose account says that Arthur was sleeping inside a hill in Gloucestershire and would awaken at the opportune moment. Despite these legends, there seems to be no prophecy in surviving Welsh poetry concerning Arthur's return, particularly in the medieval period. However, William of Malmesbury's mention in the 1120s of *antiquitas naeniarum* ('antiquity of fables'), prophesying Arthur's return, ought to mean poetry (Latin *nenia* is a mournful song or popular song), so we can only suppose that such prophetic poetry concerning Arthur did exist at that time, but has not been preserved.

V

Three Dialogue Poems

Three poems all of the same type, though doubtless of varying dates, can usefully be considered together. All three are chiefly in the three-line *englyn* metre, and have the form of dialogues, with two or more characters conversing in successive stanzas. Both 'Arthur and the Eagle' and 'The dialogue of Melwas and Gwenhwyfar' may be as early as the mid-twelfth century, though they survive only in later manuscripts; but the date is uncertain and could be later. 'Ystorya Trystan' is unlikely to be so early (perhaps of the fourteenth or fifteenth century instead), the earliest manuscript being of the sixteenth century. These poems belong partly in the tradition of the earlier *englyn* poetry, where poems in dialogue form also occur; but they are less highly worked and, in the case of 'Melwas' and 'Trystan', they also have points in common with the English ballad tradition (compare the English Arthurian ballad referred to earlier), except that the Welsh poems, as usual, are not narrative in intent.

The purpose of 'Arthur and the Eagle' is religious instruction. Arthur learns, by rather stolid questioning, that the eagle is his nephew Eliwlad, son of Madog son of Uthr – a rare instance of a paternal relative for Arthur. It is unknown whether the pre-Geoffrey tradition in Wales recognized Uthr as Arthur's father and, therefore, it is uncertain whether this detail in the poem indicates influence from

Geoffrey's HISTORY or not. Eliwlad has returned from the dead, and thus is in a position to offer special insight into the Christian life. Throughout the poem Arthur asks questions which the eagle courteously answers. This is a widely used mode of instruction, and an effective one, since even rather obvious statements of doctrine can lose some of their triteness for the listener if a third party (here Arthur) is seen to be in need of guidance. Barry Lewis has pointed out that a sixteenth-century dialogue between a *creiriwr* ('pilgrim') and Mary Magdalene of Brynbuga (the town of Usk) is remarkably similar in both form and content to the dialogue with the Eagle, the questions and answers occupying alternate *englynion* (here of four lines, so presumably later), and the pilgrim's questions being of a similarly elementary nature.

Arthur commences by establishing the identity of the eagle; when he learns that it is his dead nephew, his first reaction is to bring him back from Heaven by force of arms:

> *Yr Eryr, iaith ddiymgel:*
> *a allai neb drwy ryfel*
> *yn fyw eilwaith dy gaffel?*

> *Arthur, bendefig haelion:*
> *o chredir geiriau'r Ganon,*
> *a Duw ni thycia ymryson.*

> *(O eagle, of unhidden speech:*
> *could anyone, through battle,*
> *win you alive again?*

> *Arthur, chief of generous men:*
> *if the words of the Canon are believed,*
> *it is of no use to strive against God.)*

Arthur's reaction here probably reflects his men's speciality in rescuing prisoners – twice in CULHWCH, and again in 'Preiddiau Annwn', for instance – which was developed in chivalric romance; but that does not lessen the inappropriateness of his question.

The portrayal of Arthur in this poem is very similar to that of the saints' Lives: Arthur is well-intentioned, but not terribly bright; he needs to have the basics of the Christian life explained to him. Several of Arthur's questions are on the same elementary level as that already seen – *Ae da gan Grist y voli?* ('Is Christ glad to be praised?'); *Ae Dydbrawt y rodir y Varn?* ('Is it on Doomsday that Judgement will be given?') – reinforcing the initial impression of Arthur's slow-wittedness. The poem ends with the eagle's assertion that all will learn their place at the final reckoning (or, in some versions, with the further advice of prayer and attendance at Mass for the soul's benefit).

Some hints of Arthur's well-known links with Cornwall appear: Arthur describes the eagle as 'traversing the valley-wood of Cornwall' (*a dreigla Glyngoet Kernyw*) – probably no specific place was in the poet's mind, but merely the kind of wild habitat favoured by Arthur as well as eagles – and the eagle calls Arthur *pen kadoed Kernyw* ('chief of the hosts of Cornwall'): Sims-Williams has compared this description with the *dux bellorum* of the HISTORIA BRITTONUM. Arthur receives other military epithets, *gwryt gadarnaf* ('strongest in valour') and the like: to fit the requirements of the metre, the eagle must vary its description of Arthur in order to determine the rhymes of the stanzas.

Apart from these details, no further story emerges; the important question is why Arthur was chosen for the role of questioner in the poem. It may be that his role in some of the saints' Lives made him seem appropriate. (We can assume that the author of this poem was learned and Latin-literate.) Perhaps Arthur was used simply to provide some narrative interest, or to encourage the listener by showing that even Arthur needed elementary instruction of this kind. There may have been an earlier tradition of a wise eagle's prophecy, for Geoffrey of Monmouth refers twice to an eagle prophesying at Shaftesbury – though such a work, if it actually existed, need not have involved Arthur, of course; and our eagle does not strictly prophesy, except briefly about Doomsday. It is also worth remembering that there is a prophetic dialogue in Middle Breton between Arthur and Guinglaff, a wise man of the woods, written in about the mid-fifteenth century; the subject matter is quite different from 'Arthur and the Eagle', being historical events prophesied retrospectively (as in the early Welsh prophetic Myrddin poems). At any rate, it is tempting to suppose that something in the character of Arthur in Welsh tradition made him a suitable stooge in such situations, and this question will be examined later (see chapter IX). Although 'Arthur and the Eagle' is a learned composition, in its form of *englyn* dialogue it seems likely to have been imitating poems current in oral tradition, such as the other two to be examined in this chapter.

The poem known as 'The dialogue of Melwas and Gwenhwyfar' exists only as two partial texts (both late copies), and is obscure, either through incompleteness or through our lacking the background to the dialogue – perhaps both. The differences between the two versions are generally felt to be such as to suggest oral circulation of the poem. No introduction or context is given; our knowledge of the speakers comes from their addressing each other by name within the poem. The dialogue consists primarily of an exchange in which Melwas boasts of his martial prowess, while Gwenhwyfar contemptuously doubts it:

> *Taw, was, taw a'th salwet:*
> *onit [wyt] well na'th welet,*
> *ni ddalut Gai ar d'wythvet.*

> *Gwenhwyvar olwg hyddgan,*
> *na'm dirmic, cyd bwy bychan:*
> *mi ddaliwn Gai vy hunan.*

> *(Silence, lad, with your vileness:*
> *unless you are better than you appear,*
> *as one of eight you could not hold Cai.*

> *Gwenhwyfar, of the doe's look,*
> *do not disdain me, though I be small:*
> *I could hold Cai on my own.)*

The conversation seems to end with Gwenhwyfar suspecting that she has seen Melwas before, and his acknowledgement that this occurred in Devon (*Dyfnaint*).

Attempts to understand the dialogue have placed it in the context of the story told by Caradog in his Life of St Gildas, whereby Melwas abducted Guinevere and she was recovered by Arthur. Some version of this episode was also known to Dafydd ap Gwilym in the fourteenth century:

Ffenestr â hon yn ffunud . . .
y dôi Felwas o draserch
drwyddi . . .
gynt ger tŷ ferch Ogfran Gawr.

(A window of one form with that one . . .
through which Melwas came, from excessive love, . . .
once at the house of Ogfran the Giant's daughter.)

If read in the light of that story, the dialogue could be envisaged as an overture to the abduction: Gwenhwyfar's underestimation of Melwas's ability may have contributed to his success. That seems more likely than that the abduction was itself the previous occasion when she had seen him. Alternatively, it has been suggested that Arthur could be one of the speakers; if more than the usual two speakers are involved it is probably impossible to sort out the complexities. Apart from its relationship with Caradog's episode, the poem also finds a close echo in Chrétien's romance of Lancelot, where Guinevere is abducted by a king Meleagant (see p. 82).

The third dialogue poem, known as 'Ystorya Trystan', is concerned with Trystan and Esyllt. The legend of Trystan ('Tristan' in French legend) is generally assumed to have been originally a separate body of story which became drawn into the Arthurian cycle in the twelfth century, as part of the Matter of Britain. This poem need be no older than the fourteenth or fifteenth century; again it exists in different versions, with considerable variation between them. Some have a prose introduction, describing how Trystan and Esyllt elope to the Caledonian forest; March, the wronged husband, goes to Arthur his kinsman to demand justice. Trystan and Esyllt are surrounded in the forest, but cannot be attacked owing to Trystan's magical abilities; however, in stanzaic conversations Arthur's warriors Cai (conversing with Esyllt) and Gwalchmai (conversing with Trystan) persuade the lovers to come and submit to judgement. For Cai the conversation has an added edge, since he is himself in love with Esyllt's handmaid, Golwg Hafddydd ('Sight of a Summer's Day'); Esyllt promises him a successful suit. Arthur decrees that March and Trystan should share Esyllt, one having her while the trees should be in leaf, and one when they should be bare, with March as rightful husband to have the choice. March chooses the winter season, with its longer nights, and Esyllt, delighted, sings a closing *englyn* (this time of four lines):

> *Tri ffren sy dda i rryw,*
> *kelyn ag eiddew ag yw,*
> *a ddeilia'u [dail] yn i byw:*
> *Trystan pie fi yni fyw!*

> *(Three trees are of good kind,*
> *holly and ivy and yew,*
> *which keep their leaves while they live:*
> *Trystan shall have me while he lives!)*

Arthur's role is as an arbiter and peacekeeper, and as the leader whose warriors act as intermediaries to persuade the lovers to come out of the forest. Gwalchmai's role as tactful negotiator is his usual one, as seen in the romance of PEREDUR, for example; but Cai is not normally successful in that capacity, and to find him as a lover is even more at variance with his earlier, sharp-tongued, character.

The three poems collectively show the figure of Arthur being used in a tradition of dialogue-poetry (circulating probably in both written and oral forms) in the twelfth century or later, for purposes largely independent of the conventional Matter of Britain, but doubtless showing its influence here and there. This poetic tradition was long to continue in Welsh, and three other items of the same kind deserve mention in this context. They survive only in post-medieval versions, with no reason to be claimed as early. In one dialogue, Arthur seems to ask his sister for lodging, but she does not recognize him (hints of 'Pa ŵr yw'r porthor?', and of 'King Arthur and King Cornwall'); in a second dialogue, the dying Arthur seems to give an account of the battle of Camlan to Gwenhwyfar: *Marw Medrod, mine hayach* ('Medrod is dead, I too nearly so'); and a third poem is a lament spoken by Cai for the wounded Dillus the Bearded after the two (working together!) had been hunting the Fox of Arllechwedd (in Gwynedd), in order to bring it alive to Arthur's court (hints of CULHWCH, to which reference is made by an allusion to the hunting of Twrch Trwyth – using that form, as in CULHWCH). The evidence of 'Arthur and the Eagle', 'Melwas' and 'Ystorya Trystan', combined with these later pieces, shows that the figure of Arthur played a part in this well-established poetic tradition of *englyn* dialogues, with its roots going back to the ninth century, although there is no evidence that Arthurian dialogues were composed as early as that. We have already seen how Arthur came to play a similar, though very minor, role in the English ballad tradition.

VI

The Matter of Britain

Geoffrey of Monmouth's HISTORY OF THE KINGS OF BRITAIN has already been mentioned several times. Writing in Oxford in the 1130s, Geoffrey composed a history of Britain in the pre-English period, drawing on several known sources (including Gildas, Bede, the ninth-century HISTORIA BRITTONUM and Welsh genealogies), and possibly others, including vernacular stories (written or oral) and poetry. Geoffrey's connection with Wales is unknown, except for his name, which presumably indicates that he came from Monmouth; in Oxford he was actually known as Geoffrey 'Arthur', presumably because of his known interest in that figure of legend even before he completed his HISTORY. No evidence at all is available concerning Geoffrey's ancestry (despite modern claims that he was of Breton extraction).

Geoffrey's HISTORY was aimed primarily at a Norman audience, and it was taken up enthusiastically in literary circles in England and on the Continent; but it was also very popular in Wales. At least two reasons for his success in Wales can be suggested. Welsh readers would have recognized some of their own traditions emerging from Geoffrey's stories, albeit in modified form, and would perhaps appreciate finding those names and stories circulating among an international readership. In addition, the work celebrated both Britain as a unified kingdom (albeit one where England had primacy over Wales) and the Britons as its original inhabitants, noble and glorious – an attitude which Geoffrey shared with, and presumably obtained from, the Welsh literary background which also informed such works as the Four Branches of the Mabinogi and the poetry of the earliest Gogynfeirdd or their now-lost predecessors. This shared attitude would have added to the appeal of Geoffrey's work for the Welsh, even though he also denigrated the latter-day Welsh as unworthy heirs to the noble British tradition, showing the Bretons in a more favourable light. (There was a political reason for this, in that the Bretons were in favour with the Norman rulers; Geoffrey thus enabled the English kings later to turn the ideal of a politically unified Britain against their immediate neighbours in Wales and Scotland.) Geoffrey's HISTORY belongs in a book on the Welsh Arthurian legend, both because his sources included Welsh legend and because of the enthusiastic reception which his work had in Wales.

Arthur was the most glorious of the kings whom Geoffrey's HISTORY purports to document, and he thus provides the climax to the work. For the first time we have a complete life history for Arthur, from birth to death, not *a* story of Arthur but *the* story. It may be doubted whether anyone had thought of telling this previously. For the first time, too, Arthur became fully involved in the Welsh literary and political concept of a unified Britain, though Geoffrey may have developed that out of his title in CULHWCH, 'chief of the lords of this island'. Many of the later elements of the international Arthurian legend appear for the first time in Geoffrey's work: his irregular conception at Tintagel by Uther Pendragon and Igerna; his glorious and idealized reign as king; Modred's treachery and his adultery with Guinevere, resulting in the final battle of Camlan; Arthur's fatal wounding there and his removal to the isle of Avallon. (Well-known elements notably lacking, and not found until later, include the sword in the stone, Camelot, the Round Table and the Holy Grail; these were mostly added in French romances of the thirteenth century.) Geoffrey also introduced the figure of Merlin into the legend, as a prophet and magician; he was freely derived from the Welsh legends of Myrddin, but in Welsh those legends were separate from the Arthurian legend, and largely remained so.

In what was probably Geoffrey's own contribution to the legend, Arthur becomes an international warlord on a magnificent scale. Drawing his inspiration perhaps from Welsh stories of Arthur's adventures abroad (as in the porter's reminiscences in CULHWCH), and certainly from the growing international legend of Alexander, Geoffrey makes Arthur first bring the Saxons under control, then conquer Scotland, Ireland and Iceland; after twelve years' rule, with knights coming from afar to join his court, Arthur goes on to conquer Norway, Denmark and Gaul. After a further nine years he is imperially crowned in a splendid ceremony at Caerleon. At this point the Roman emperor feels threatened by his success and sends for him.

In response Arthur again takes an army to the Continent. In an episode atmospherically reminiscent of CULHWCH, on Mont St Michel he slays a giant who has abducted and killed a Breton princess, and then successfully engages with the Roman armies. He crosses the Alps and is about to attack Rome

74

itself when he receives news that his nephew Modred, whom he has left in charge in Britain, has seized the crown, is adulterously cohabiting with Guinevere, and has asked the Continental Saxons for military aid. Arthur returns hastily to Britain, pursues Modred to Cornwall and there fights and kills him at the River *Camblanus*, himself receiving a fatal wound in the process. Geoffrey evidently knew Camlan from Welsh sources and chose to locate it in Cornwall. Arthur was, for Geoffrey, closely associated with Cornwall, whether because of *Kelli wic* or for other reasons; however, he located Arthur's court at Caerleon-on-Usk instead, presumably because of its impressive Roman remains, and perhaps out of local pride in his home district of Monmouth. After the battle Arthur, though mortally wounded, is taken to Avallon *to have his wounds healed* – probably a coy reference to the legend of his return. After his reign the British resistance to the Saxons soon crumbles, partly through internal discord, serving to emphasize Arthur's own achievement.

Geoffrey's History forms the most significant milestone in the development of Arthurian litera-ture, for he gave the legend both the shape that it was to have ever after and the international literary currency which has endured to this day. One difficult topic in the development of the Arthurian legend is the relationship, if any, between Geoffrey's History and Culhwch. The two share several narrative details, such as the saints of Ireland coming to ask Arthur's protection when he lands there to hunt the Twrch (Culhwch) and the clergy of Scotland begging mercy from Arthur after he had conquered their country (Geoffrey); also the parallel of both the Twrch and Modred heading for Cornwall and Arthur's particular horror at that development. Although CULHWCH is generally dated to 'around 1100', the development of Welsh prose in the twelfth century is insufficiently attested to deny categorically that the tale must be earlier than Geoffrey's HISTORY. Nevertheless, the fundamental difference between the two works remains the portrayal of Arthur, the supernatural, folklore atmosphere of CULHWCH contrasting with Geoffrey's regal splendour. However, it is clear that the portrayal of Arthur in CULHWCH, and also the hunting of the Twrch Trwyth, go back centuries earlier than Geoffrey's HISTORY, so the dating of CULHWCH, whether earlier than the HISTORY or not, does not fundamentally affect our view of the developing figure of Arthur.

There is some evidence that Arthurian stories were already popular on the Continent before Geoffrey's HISTORY was completed in about 1138. This may partly account for the immediate success that his work enjoyed there as well as in England. But Geoffrey's HISTORY seems to have made a difference, in that it apparently rendered these Arthurian stories more acceptable in courtly circles, perhaps because he had *by means of the Latin language cloaked the fables about Arthur in the respectable name of history,* as William of Newburgh put it later in the century. At any rate, it was about thirty years after Geoffrey wrote his HISTORY that the new French literary genre of romances began to embrace stories centred on King Arthur's court, and the probability is that Geoffrey's HISTORY played a catalytic role in bringing about this new literary form of Arthurian romance, which was to enjoy popularity throughout western Europe for three centuries. The name for the whole body of legend was the Matter of Britain, by analogy with the Matter of Rome (which paradoxically was mainly about the Greek legends of Troy and the conquests of Alexander) and the Matter of France, concerned with Charlemagne and Roland. It is because of this international popularity throughout Europe in the late Middle Ages that the legend of Arthur is so well known today, and the form in which it is known is irremediably affected by Geoffrey's work.

The salient features of Arthurian romances in their early years were: concentration upon an individual knight and his development, particularly in the matter of learning to live up to the chivalric ideal; to that end, a common plot whereby the knight travels forth, seeking challenges which will serve to build his character (this later became diverted into the Quest for the Holy Grail, an attempt to regain a lost spiritual ideal); and a close interest in human relationships, particularly in love and the individual knight's dealings with women. King Arthur himself often plays little part, although these are 'Arthurian romances' in the true sense of the term. His court was merely the framework into which the adventures of particular knights were fitted, working within a set of common assumptions and conventions. In the work of Chrétien de Troyes (c. 1160–90) King Arthur's court became, and was later to remain, a flawed ideal, or an ideal which was impossible to attain. In later romances the infidelity of Queen Guinevere with Lancelot, and Arthur's own incestuous relationship with his half-sister which produced the traitor Mordred, constituted the flaw at the centre of this otherwise glorious and idealistic micro-society.

The three Welsh Romances, GERAINT, OWAIN and

PEREDUR, fit into this common pattern. Each tells the story of a single knight of Arthur's court and charts his development, particularly in the matter of reconciling the opposing requirements of marriage and prowess at arms; and each does so by means of the standard plot of having the knight travel forth through unknown lands, finding challenges by which to prove himself. Each romance thus corresponds closely in plot to one of Chrétien's romances, too closely for there not to be a genetic relationship. The connection between the two groups has been much discussed, but the discussion seems destined to remain inconclusive. What is clear, however, is that whatever the relationship between the two groups, all three Welsh tales show pervasive influence from this new genre, not only in matters of incidental detail (such as the portcullis in OWAIN, the castles in PEREDUR and the tournament in GERAINT; the ladies' names Luned and Enid; and the concept of knighthood which shapes all three tales) but, more fundamentally, in the matter of design and construction, as outlined above. In other words, their basic structure shows these tales to be Welsh examples of works composed within the new French genre. For this reason they are unlikely to have been composed before the thirteenth century, although GERAINT, at least, must date from early in that century, since fragments of the tale survive in manuscripts from soon after that date; much of PEREDUR also exists in a thirteenth-century manuscript. It is still unclear to what extent the three tales should be considered a group: although they clearly belong together in content, and in the role of Arthur within each one, critics have detected differences of style and language which suggest that the three were composed by different authors, or by different translators if that was how they came into being.

However, although these works were evidently composed within the new genre of the romance, the matter is not so straightforward. The Welsh tales follow the regular pattern of the genre, but they do not display the close interest in characterization, development and human relationships which that pattern is designed to serve. As in the Four Branches, characterization is left to be read between the lines. The Welsh romances are thus structured as if written within the same new genre as Chrétien's romances, but omitting the primary purpose of that genre.

In addition, the Welsh romances differ fundamentally from other tales within the 'Mabinogion' in their geographical perspective. In this sense they can be said to have a 'foreign' outlook compared with other Welsh tales. This manifests itself in their vagueness of location, which forms a sharp contrast with the detailed wealth of place-names found in the Four Branches and CULHWCH. Caerleon-on-Usk is the name of Arthur's court in all three romances, evidently following Geoffrey's HISTORY; but, apart from that, OWAIN and PEREDUR contain almost no place-names at all, except that PEREDUR mentions Gloucester (*Kaer Loyw*) as the home of the Nine Witches, and also a few exotic or obviously fictional places such as India, Constantinople and *Y Cruc Galarus* ('The Dolorous Mound'). GERAINT contains a little more geography, but it is still minimal: the author displays enough knowledge of south-east Wales to know that Cardiff and the Forest of Dean are not far from Caerleon, and that the Forest is reached by crossing the River Usk. These would have been well-known places, and the degree of geographical knowledge is still much slighter than the informative precision of CULHWCH and the Four Branches.

In all three stories, all geographic precision ceases when the knight's wandering commences: the important point about the adventures is not where they occur, but that it is elsewhere, away from Arthur's court, and that this 'elsewhere' is evidently the appropriate setting for the supernatural and other encounters which take place. (In GERAINT there is mention of *Lloegr* ('England') at the start of his wanderings, but thereafter even this precision lapses.) This is Britain seen from a Continental perspective – much as Africa or South America might have been construed in a European story of the seventeenth century. The geographical vagueness of the three tales, which even leaves us unsure whether the adventures are envisaged as occurring in Wales or in Britain at all, is one of the features which make the atmosphere of the three romances so different from that of the other Mabinogion stories.

The character of Arthur is another feature which the Welsh romances share with the French ones; his role contrasts markedly with that seen in the Welsh Arthurian material examined earlier. Arthur is described as an emperor (*amherawdyr*) in all three tales, again showing the influence of Geoffrey of Monmouth: compare the use of that term in the *englyn* poem about Geraint and Prydydd y Moch's mention of Arthur alongside Alexander and Julius Caesar. In keeping with his new status, Arthur here has a dignity and a sense of responsibility which are generally lacking in the earlier material, especially CULHWCH. He is worried and distressed by the absence of one of his knights, and concerned for their health when they are wounded. He rules as a lord, not as first among equals as CULHWCH's Arthur does. It has been suggested that the Arthur of the

Romances is the 'Arthur of CULHWCH grown old' (we might almost say 'grown-up'). He is on his way to becoming the *roi fainéant* of later Continental literature, the 'do-nothing king' whose inactivity and acquiescence constituted a central flaw in his otherwise ideal society. This acquiescence is well seen in PEREDUR, where Arthur and his knights fail to respond to the deliberate insult done to Gwenhwyfar by an unknown knight, but leave it to the newly arrived Peredur to avenge it. The insult to Gwenhwyfar in GERAINT (actually to her maidservant) is not so clear-cut, since it does not occur in Arthur's presence; but again it is left to Geraint to avenge it, and the king is remarkably placatory when the offending knight arrives, beaten by Geraint, at his court.

However, Arthur is not altogether passive: in all three romances he does ride forth – to go hunting in PEREDUR and in GERAINT, where he himself kills the white hart, and to search for the wandering knight in PEREDUR and OWAIN; in the latter tale he actually dresses for combat against the Black Knight (the unrecognized Owain), although he never fights, being forestalled by Gwalchmai. Moreover, not all of Arthur's treatment is consistent with his royal dignity and stature. A touch of humour, at Arthur's expense, seems to appear at the beginning of OWAIN, with the homeliness of a pile of green rushes as his seat (*ar demyl o irvrwyn*), incongruous among the luxurious finery of imperial power; it appears again when Arthur falls asleep while waiting for dinner, during Cynon's telling of his tale, and then wakes up and asks whether he has slept at all (*deffroi a oruc Arthur, a gofyn a gysgassei hayach*). There may be a similar touch of incongruous humour in GERAINT, where Arthur receives a reproof from his own forester for not recognizing him, and possibly also when Gwenhwyfar misses the hunt of the white hart through oversleeping, although Arthur had promised that she should witness it.

The lack of interest in the actions of Arthur himself conforms with the Continental romances, where the interest is centred on the individual knight and his development; but the homely and humorous touches recall the Arthur of CULHWCH or the saints' Lives. It is tempting to wonder whether the author of OWAIN, and maybe that of GERAINT, while building his tale around the established Continental (post-Geoffrey) image of Arthur as a magnificent emperor, could not resist alluding occasionally to the earlier, Welsh image of a more homely figure, humorously undignified at times. We shall return to this point later, in chapter IX.

In passing, it may be suggested that the closest we can get to the original Welsh material lying behind a French Arthurian romance may, paradoxically, occur in the case of Chrétien's LANCELOT, where two Welsh pieces already examined – the Glastonbury episode in Caradog's Life of Gildas and the dialogue between Melwas and Gwenhwyfar – demonstrate a Welsh legend of Gwenhwyfar's abduction. It must have been this legend – not necessarily the written materials that we have, but perhaps disparate allusions of a similar kind – which Chrétien, or his predecessor, used and assimilated to the new genre, producing the existing romance. This may give us an idea of the kind of lost Welsh legends (and their form) which we might envisage as providing the background to the existing romances of Yvain, Erec and Perceval, and how those materials were developed in the hands of the romancers.

In addition to these three Welsh romances, which either were composed within the new foreign genre or were free renderings of such romances, close translations of Arthurian material were made into Welsh. The Latin text of Geoffrey's HISTORY OF THE KINGS OF BRITAIN was translated into several languages, including Old French (by Wace in the 1150s, doubtless boosting the promotion of Arthur which Geoffrey's own work had provided in France), early Middle English (by Layamon in *c*. 1200) and Old Norse. The popularity of Geoffrey's work in Wales ensured that his HISTORY was also translated into Welsh, as BRUT Y BRENHINEDD ('The *Brut* of the kings', from the name of Brutus, Geoffrey's eponymous first founder of the British kingdom): *Brut* henceforth became a general Welsh term for any chronicle. It is recognized that three separate Welsh versions of Geoffrey's HISTORY were made in the thirteenth century, with some cross-influence between them, and a further two in the fourteenth.

The Welsh translations of Geoffrey's HISTORY remain on the whole rather faithful to their Latin original, such was the authority in which that was held. Differences lie primarily in the occasional insertion of additional material (presumed to be from Welsh tradition), in the rendering of Geoffrey's Latinized place-names and personal names (which often appeared in well-turned pseudo-ancient forms, such as *Cassibellanus* and *Estrildis*) back into their vernacular originals or into their assumed Welsh equivalents (Caswallawn, Esyllt), and sometimes in an attempt to iron out an inconsistency when Geoffrey's imagination had produced a story glaringly at variance with the Welsh traditions which formed part of his inspiration. Because of this general closeness to their original, the translations do not show anything notable in the figure of Arthur himself; their importance for our purpose lies rather in the acceptance into the Welsh vernacular, as a legitimate part of the literary tradition, of Geoffrey's new image of Arthur as a European emperor, with his magnificent court, so different from the Robin-Hood-like *Kelli wic* of earlier stories. In many respects Geoffrey's portrayal fitted well with the existing tradition: he had made use of Cai and Bedwyr (*Kaius, Beduerus*) as Arthur's close companions, notably in the attack upon the giant of Mont St Michel and the subsequent campaign in France; and their appearance in the Welsh Bruts would have seemed perfectly natural to Welsh readers.

One of the most important effects of Geoffrey's work in Welsh literature was on the Welsh Triads, because his influence there had a repercussive effect on other literary works. The Triads were a learned classification of storytelling lore, originally made presumably for the purpose of instruction or memorization, but taking on a life of their own as a collection of learned material. The lore is classified mostly by means of characters who had a feature in common (for example, no. 2, 'Three Generous Men of the Island of Britain: Nudd the Generous son of Senyllt, Mordaf the Generous son of Serwan, and Rhydderch the Generous son of Tudwal Tudglyd'; compare Prydydd y Moch's poetic use of this triad, p. 53), or sometimes by means of an animal or abstract idea ('Three Concealments and Three Disclosures of the Island of Britain').

The earliest text of the Triads dates from the thirteenth century, but it is judged that this Early Version (nos 1–46) goes back some century or more before that. In effect, the Triads may have constituted a 'Matter of Britain' even before that became an established concept internationally. Later versions, from the fourteenth century, incorporate alterations and additions. These later versions take more account of Geoffrey's HISTORY than the Early Version. For instance, instead of naming 'Three . . . of the Island of Britain', some of the later Triads name instead 'Three . . . of Arthur's court', as if Arthur's court now stood for all that was significant in legendary Britain. However, this difference between the earlier and later versions is perhaps one of degree rather than kind, for even in the Early Version a possible influence of Geoffrey's work may occasionally be detectable. The very first triad, 'Three Tribal Thrones of the Island of Britain', cites three royal seats of Arthur as *Penn teyrned* ('chief of lords') (at *Mynyw* or St David's, *Kelli Wic* in Cornwall, and the unknown *Penn Ryonedd* in the North); Arthur's title repeats that given him in CULHWCH. Although the phrase need not itself be due to Geoffrey's HISTORY (indeed, in CULHWCH it is assumed not to be), the prominent position of this Triad, and its use of Arthur's name to promote a political cause of the mid-twelfth century (the promotion of St David's), are suggestive of Geoffrey's influence. This Triad may be an accretion to the Early Version, even though it appears in the earliest manuscript; a similar possible influence is seen in the title of no. 9, 'Tri Unben Llys Arthur' ('Three Chieftains of Arthur's Court'), where Arthur's court replaces the Island of Britain, as often in later triads; surprisingly, the three chieftains named are virtually unknown characters, ones merely mentioned as followers of Arthur in CULHWCH and RHONABWY (Gobrwy son of Echel Mighty-Thigh, Cadrieith son of Porthawr Gadw, and Ffleudwr Fflam).

Arthur himself is named in the Early Version as one of 'Tri Overveird Enys Prydein' ('Three Frivolous Bards of the Island of Britain', no. 12); the category is obscure, but Arthur's *englyn* in CULHWCH which offended Cai may illustrate that aspect of his character, and his opening words in the dialogue with the Eagle, *Es ryfedaf kann wyf bard* ('I wonder, since I am a poet'), may also serve to explain it. He is also named as one of 'Tri Ruduoavc Enys Prydein' ('Three Red-ravaging Ones of the Island of Britain', no. 20), presumably intended as a compliment. In 'Tri Hael' ('Three Generous Men', no. 2), Arthur is named afterwards as being even more generous than the three generous men themselves; as noted above, Prydydd y Moch, composing before 1200, quoted the triad in this extended form. Arthur's son Llachau is named as one of 'Tri Deifnyawc Enys Prydein' ('Three Endowed Men', no. 4; another of the three was Gwalchmai) – presumably denoting an entitlement to rule. Finally within the Early Version, Arthur plays a subsidiary role in 'Tri Gwrdueichyat Enys Prydein' ('Three Mighty-swineherds of Britain', no. 26), in which Drystan (Trystan) guards March's pigs while the actual swineherd takes a message to Esyllt: *And Arthur trying to get one pig from them, whether by trickery or force, and he could not.* In later versions of this triad Cai and Bedwyr were added in support of Arthur.

In later texts of the Triads, Arthur was occasionally added to a Triad which occurs without him in the

Early Version, either by making the Triad 'Three . . . of Arthur's Court' (instead of 'the Island of Britain'), or in some other way. The most interesting instance is in 'Tri Matkud Ynys Prydein' ('Three Fortunate Concealments of Britain', no. 37): one of these concealments was the head of Bendigeidfran son of Llŷr, which, as the Second Branch of the Mabinogi relates, was hidden in the White Hill in London to prevent any oppression coming to this island. The Red Book of Hergest (*c.* 1400) adds to the Triad that Arthur himself disclosed the head again, *because he did not like this island to be protected by anyone's strength other than his own.* Rather than referring to an arrogant or darker side of Arthur, as has been suggested, this wayward act perhaps arose from his childish, petulant tendency which has already been noted in some of the earlier references, but which Geoffrey dispensed with. Arthur's role as protector of this island, comparable with Fionn's similar role in Ireland, goes back to the ninth-century List of Battles, but was probably developed in the twelfth century: the Unknown Grave mentioned by William of Malmesbury, earlier than Geoffrey's HISTORY, is linked to that role, since it implies the Prophesied Return; the imperial role in which Geoffrey cast Arthur may have given the concept a further boost, though still not sufficiently to earn him a place in the extant prophetic poetry.

Because of the greater influence of Geoffrey's HISTORY in the later versions of the Triads, there are references particularly to Medrawd (as Arthur's rival), Camlan and Gwenhwyfar – notably to the three in combination with one another. Neither Medrawd nor Gwenhwyfar appears in the Early Version, and Camlan only once, linked with an

Anglo-Norman name (and without that of Arthur). Although each of the three elements existed earlier in Welsh tradition, it was the combination of the three names which gained much greater prominence in Welsh literature as a result of Geoffrey's work. One of 'Teir Gvith Baluavt Ynys Prydein' ('Three Harmful Blows', no. 53), was that struck upon Gwenhwyfar by Gwenhwyfach, because it caused the Battle of Camlan; Medrawd's ravaging of Arthur's court and a blow that he too struck upon Gwenhwyfar are cited in 'Teir Drut Heirua' ('Three Unrestrained Ravagings', no. 54); and in 'Tri Anuat Gyghor' ('Three Unfortunate Counsels', no. 59), Arthur's triple division of his soldiers at Camlan is cited, presumably because it caused his defeat. These triads all seem to refer to unknown traditions concerning Camlan; the traditions were presumably independent of Geoffrey's HISTORY, but their importance was perhaps increased by the prominence which he gave to that battle.

The reception of Geoffrey's HISTORY in Wales, as elsewhere, was not altogether favourable, and it is worth mentioning the story which Gerald of Wales told of a madman in Caerleon (the place can hardly be a coincidence), whose evil spirits were expelled by placing a copy of St John's Gospel on his chest; but, says Gerald, if the Gospel was replaced with Geoffrey's HISTORY, the devils came swarming back, more vigorous than before. Nevertheless, despite the doubts of Gerald and a few others, the enduring influence of Geoffrey's book testifies to its qualities, which the literary world in Wales had even more reason to appreciate than those elsewhere.

Geoffrey's HISTORY was not the only Arthurian work

translated into Welsh. In the first quarter of the thirteenth century a series of French prose romances was composed. The initial inspiration came from the desire to complete Chrétien's PERCEVAL, which he had left unfinished in *c.* 1190; the quest of King Arthur's knights for the Holy Grail became the central focus. These prose romances thus were more spiritual and allegorical in intent, contrasting with those of Chrétien which had concentrated instead on human character and relationships. Two of these prose romances were translated into Welsh, the QUESTE DEL SAINT GRAAL and PERLESVAUS, the two known collectively as YSTORYAEU SEINT GREAL ('The Stories of the Holy Grail'), which is in two sections according to its two French originals. The translation was made probably in the late fourteenth century.

The Welsh text remains faithfully close to its French originals, so the portrayal of Arthur seen here is effectively a thirteenth-century French one. Both sections are concerned chiefly with the adventures of three knights, Paredur, Galaath and Bwrt in the first, and Paredur, Lawnslot and Gwalchmai in the second; however, Arthur's role is very different in the two parts, reflecting his roles in the two original romances. In the first he appears only at the beginning and end. At the start he regrets the departure of his knights on their quest, knowing that some will never return and that this signifies the end of the Order of the Round Table:

'Lawnslot', heb yr Arthur, 'nyt oed ryued im dristau, kany wydywn yn yr holl vyt brenhin Cristawn kyn amlet y vilwyr da a'e varchogyon aruawc ac yttoedwn i hediw y bore.'

('Lancelot', said Arthur, 'it were no wonder for me to grieve, for

I should not know in the whole world a Christian king with so many good soldiers and armed knights as I was this morning.')

Similarly, at the very end of the Quest, when Bwrt returned to Arthur's court to report the encounter of the three knights with the Grail, Arthur ordered his account to be written down.

Arthur's role in the second part, translated from the prose *Perlesvaus*, is very different. He takes an active part in campaigns, and jousts in a tournament:

Ac yn y twrneimant y trawssant wy yll tri megys llewot a dianghei oc eu cadwyneu . . . ac ny chyvaruu yn y dyd hwnnw neb a'r brenhin neb ny's bwryei y lawr neu ynteu a gollei y daryan.

(*And in the tournament they all three* [Arthur, Lawnslot and Gwalchmai] *struck like lions escaping from their chains . . . and that day nobody met with the king whom he did not hurl down, or else who lost his shield.*)

Several episodes take place at Arthur's court at Caerleon, and there is overt reference to the love of Gwenhwyfar and Lawnslot. Two further themes in this second section are Cai's killing of Arthur's son Llachau (named at first as Loawt, imitating Loholt in the French original, but thereafter as Llachau), with Cai's consequent exile in Brittany and his hostility to Arthur, reminiscent of the same theme in CULHWCH, though for different reasons; and Arthur's misplaced trust in the treacherous *Briant o'r Ynyssed* ('Brian of the Isles'), showing the kind of misjudgement which weakened his rule in later legend. Camelot appears, probably for the first time in Welsh (*Castell Camalot*), though it is here a castle of Paredur's mother, not of Arthur.

Overall, then, the figure of Arthur found in Y SEINT GREAL, though differing between the two sections, shows that the French concepts of Arthur could comfortably be accommodated in Welsh in the late fourteenth century. However, for all the faithfulness of this translation, Lloyd-Morgan has pointed out that the translator did somewhat shorten the originals, particularly some of the discussions of chivalry and the allegorical explanations: his interest was in the adventures and the stories themselves, rather than analyses of abstract problems. It is notable that this relationship of the Welsh translation to its French originals is similar to that of the three Welsh Romances compared with their counterparts by Chrétien, whereby the Welsh tales concentrate upon the adventures themselves rather than the more abstract ideas which interested Chrétien.

Before 1400 a Welsh translation had also been made of the French narrative telling how Arthur pulled the sword out of the stone, thus proving his right to the throne of Britain despite the resistance of the barons and the false claim of his foster-brother Cai. This story came from the French Prose Merlin, and again the translation is close, with some abridgement and the substitution of Welsh names (such as Myrddin) for the French ones. As with the Grail romances, the new developments were able to be harmonized with Welsh tradition, and also with Geoffrey's HISTORY, to which the story makes specific reference.

In the fifteenth century this blended Continental–Welsh Arthur continued his literary career. One interesting result of the blend was a short piece, 'The twenty-four knights of Arthur's court'. In this tract, effectively a group of eight Triads, the knights are grouped in threes according to their special skills or characteristics. Some characters came straight from the list of Arthur's warriors in CULHWCH, for example 'Three offensive knights' of Arthur's court, who could not be refused anything, Morvran ap Tegid, Sanddef Bryd Angel ('Angel-face') and Glewlwyd Gavaelvawr; others came from the romances, such as 'Three virgin knights', Bwrt, Peredur and Galath. This mixture of older and imported figures at Arthur's court shows how thoroughly the two traditions were able to complement one another.

It has been noted earlier that some aspects of romantic Arthurian literature were already present in Welsh tradition before Geoffrey: Arthur's wide geographical range, seeds of the later chivalric code of the Round Table (as shown by Arthur's own remark in CULHWCH concerning the honour of his court, the remark of Cai and Bedwyr in the Life of St Cadog concerning their duties, and the recurrent theme of rescuing prisoners), and the emphasis upon the figures surrounding Arthur rather than Arthur himself. Geoffrey himself refers once to the knights' desire for winning the ladies' approbation, which later formed an important dimension of their desire for martial glory – one of the major differences between a heroic and a chivalric code of honour. But these themes were naturally developed in very different directions in the hands of Continental romancers.

The works examined in this section, notably the three Romances and the obviously translated works, BRUT Y BRENHINEDD and Y SEINT GREAL, show Wales partaking in the European literary culture of the period. This is also shown by other, non-Arthurian, translations into Welsh such as YSTORYA DE CAROLO MAGNO (the Charlemagne legend) and YSTORYA BOWN DE HAMTWN (the romance of Bevis of Hampton). The difference, in Wales, was that the Matter of Britain struck a particular chord because of its partial derivation from older Welsh legends. However, apart from the few hints in the three Romances, the international portrayal of Arthur himself seems rapidly to have become dominant in Wales, and little trace of the older Welsh Arthur emerges from these works written in the European mould. The two blended anyway in such a manner that it might be meaningless to distinguish one from the other: we have already seen that medieval Welsh authors adopted a liberal attitude towards variations and inconsistencies. But Wales also continued to employ its own distinctive literary forms, and Arthur, in this blend of indigenous and international figure, naturally appeared there too. These are the works to be examined in the next chapter.

VII

The Continuing Tradition

THE DREAM OF RHONABWY has been variously dated
between the late twelfth and the late fourteenth
century. No work, except possibly the GODODDIN,
better exemplifies our difficulties in interpreting the
anonymous works of Medieval Welsh literature
through not being able to date them precisely. The
difficulty is increased by the pointlessness of the tale,
because of its lack of a narrative thread: Rhonabwy
falls asleep in a filthy hall while journeying to make
peace between warring brothers in Powys, Madog
ap Maredudd (died 1160, the last king of Powys) and
Iorwerth. He dreams of the prelude to Arthur's
battle of Badon, but Arthur seems only interested in
playing *gwyddbwyll* (a board-game) against his own
soldier Owain ab Urien. Meanwhile, Arthur's men
and Owain's ravens are slaughtering each other out
of sight. Arthur ends the board-game by crushing
the pieces, and Rhonabwy wakes up.

Critics are agreed concerning the problems of understanding this piece. Slotkin has pointed out, first,
that the DREAM is strikingly unlike most dreams in
medieval literature, in that it contains no articulated
lesson or prophecy for the frame in which it occurs,
nor do we return to that frame after Rhonabwy
awakens – it is instead much more like an actual
dream in its illogical and topsy-turvy world; and,
second, that the lack of events is partly due to the
fact that time runs backwards: Rhonabwy's guide in

the DREAM, Iddawg, has completed seven years of penance for causing Arthur's final battle of Camlan, yet the battle of Badon is about to take place. It has been pointed out that the cryptic remark at the end

No-one, neither poet nor storyteller, knows the Dream without a book, because of all the colours upon the horses and the amount of varied colour upon the weapons and their harnesses, upon the valuable clothes and the precious stones

is misleading, both because RHONABWY would certainly be no harder to remember than, say, PEREDUR or GERAINT, and because the formulaic nature of the descriptions is actually suited to memorization. The remark pointedly draws attention to those very descriptions which serve to hinder the action, or to disguise the lack of it.

Within the DREAM, Arthur himself is a mockery of the noble king of romance: he is described as an *amherawdyr*, as in the three Romances and elsewhere, and is surrounded by the luxuries of that position; but he carries the inactivity of the romantic Arthur to the extreme, by continuing to play *gwyddbwyll* while his warriors are slaughtered off-stage. Moreover, he seems to know that he is taking part in a dream, or at least is not in his own era. Immediately on meeting Rhonabwy and his companions, Arthur refers to them as *y dynyon bychein hynny* ('those little men'), presumably because of the common folklore tradition of Arthur and his men having the stature of giants; he subsequently explains his wry smile:

'Nyt chwerthin a wnaf, namyn truanet gennyf vot dynyon ky vawhet a hynn yn gwarchadw yr ynys honn gwedy gwyr kystal ac a'e gwarchetwis gynt.'

('I am not laughing, but am so sad that men as vile as these should be guarding this island, after men as good as those who guarded it formerly.')

The portrayal of Arthur in this tale contains elements both from earlier Welsh literature and from post-Geoffrey romance. Arthur has no patronym (neither does Rhonabwy), and his court (unnamed) is in Cornwall, as in CULHWCH; but Cadwr earl of Cornwall is his right-hand man, as in Geoffrey's HISTORY. March ap Meirchiawn, here king of Llychlyn (Scandinavia), is said to be Arthur's cousin, as in the story framing the Trystan dialogue. Considering Arthur's lack of clear ancestry (indeed, of any ancestry at all) in early Welsh literature, the number of cousins attributed to him in various texts is surprising, and it seems to have been commonplace to link notable figures with him in this conveniently vague way. RHONABWY also gives a list of forty-one counsellors (*kyghorwyr*) of Arthur's court; the list has much in common with the longer list of warriors in CULHWCH and the shorter list of eighteen courtiers in GERAINT, although, unlike the two earlier texts, the list in RHONABWY does include Llachau son of Arthur – perhaps as a result of his continuing popularity among the poets of the twelfth century and later.

Commentators agree that RHONABWY is a self-consciously literary, bookish, work, indeed a satire or parody – if only because no other purpose can be imagined; but they have been less sure what its target is. If it is a satire, with a political or social message, then one recent critic has suggested that it was written soon after 1216 and was aimed against Llywelyn ab Iorwerth (Llywelyn the Great, died 1240), offering in warning an unfavourable comparison with another leader of a united Wales. However, any precise message was well disguised, to have escaped identification for so long.

If the piece is a parody, then romantic Arthurian literature is presumably its object. The lengthy descriptions might be intended to illustrate the danger of allowing such set pieces too great a role in a story. There is also a jibe against the Gogynfeirdd, in the mention of an ode sung in praise of Arthur:

Nachaf ueird yn dyuot y datkanu kerd y Arthur; ac nyt oed dyn a adnapei y gerd honno, namyn Kadyrieith ehun, eithyr y uot yn uolyant y Arthur.

(Behold, poets coming to recite a poem to Arthur; and there was nobody who recognized that poem, only Cadrieith himself, except that it was praise for Arthur.)

However, this remark seems to be more a passing sideswipe than showing the main target of the humour.

Even Rhonabwy's name is problematical, not being found other than for this 'hero'. It was perhaps invented for the story, by analogy with other names in *-abwy*, such as Gwernabwy. The poet Madog Dwygraig, in about 1370–80, referred to Rhonabwy in a poem to Morgan ap Llywelyn:

> *Ry aniben wyf, eil Ronabwy,*
> *ryw vreudwydyd moel, koel keladwy.*

> *(I am too dilatory, another Rhonabwy,*
> *some mere dreamer – secret portent!)*

97

This clearly refers to the DREAM: perhaps Madog was alluding topically to a work recently composed and circulated.

The problems of interpretation are greatly lessened if we reclassify the work. The inclusion of this tale among the Mabinogion is misleading. In the Red Book of Hergest (*c.* 1400), the sole manuscript containing this story, RHONABWY is not placed alongside the other ten tales of the Mabinogion, which do appear together, both here and in the earlier White Book of Rhydderch. The satirical or parodic tone and the inconsequential plot set the DREAM apart from the Mabinogion proper. Both Bollard and Lloyd-Morgan have suggested that it is a different sort of text altogether, a rhetorical composition of a kind with the later AREITHIAU PROS (the 'prose rhetorics').

Although the earliest manuscript containing AREITH-IAU is of the sixteenth century, one piece attributed to the fourteenth-century poet Iolo Goch is of particular relevance here, being a parody of CULHWCH; though it does not mention Arthur himself, it contains several direct allusions to CULHWCH, as well as further echoes of both style and content (see p. 20). The similarities between this short piece and RHONABWY lie in its cursory historical setting, its flowery rhetorical descriptions and the inconclusive nature of its story. (A spotty youth of Gwynedd sends a lad to Powys to woo a princess on his behalf; she sets impossible conditions, like Ysbaddaden, and the lad returns with those answers: the end.) Lloyd-Morgan has also compared RHONABWY with two other AREITHIAU, one containing an account of unpleasant lodgings, of which the rhetorical description is an end in itself (as is that of the fine clothing in RHONABWY), and another, attributed to the fourteenth-century poet Gruffudd ab Adda ap Dafydd, offering a dream-vision of a river with different plants and animals on either side (like the sheep in PEREDUR) and a battle involving two flocks of ravens. If we regard RHONABWY as an early, and rather long, example of an ARAITH, then its precedence of rhetoric over action makes good sense. It would then be misguided to read too much into its contents, though it might still carry a satirical message against civil strife, or a parodic dig at the expense of late-medieval Arthurian romance.

References to Arthur and his world continued to be made by the poets in the later Middle Ages. In the later thirteenth century, the poet Bleddyn Fardd showed a particular fondness for Arthurian allusions. In one of his two elegies for Llywelyn ap Gruffudd (Llywelyn the Last, died 1282) he compared Llywelyn with Arthur (also with another national hero, Bendigeidfran), referring to Arthur as an *amerodr* ('emperor'). In other poems he referred separately to Llachau's death (telling us, which we do not learn elsewhere, that he was slain *below Llech Ysgar* – perhaps on Crickheath Hill south of Oswestry, in Shropshire), to Peredur, Geraint and Owain, and to the ever-popular Elifri. Gruffudd ab yr Ynad Coch in turn, in his elegy for Llywelyn the Last, compared the skirmish in which he was killed with the battle of Camlan, implying that the two were comparable in their far-reaching effects:

> *Llawer llef druan, ual ban vu Gamlan,*
> *llawer deigyr dros rann gwedy r'greinyaw.*
>
> (*Many a pitiful voice, as when Camlan occurred,*
> *many a tear flooding down over cheek.*)

For the most part the Arthurian references at this period do not show whether it was the Arthur of CULHWCH or the emperor of romance that was evoked – probably a mixture of the two. But Bleddyn Fardd also mentioned Caerleon, *y lle teccaf* ('the fairest place'), possibly an allusion to it as the location of Arthur's court.

However, as could be expected, the indigenous images of Arthur's world proved persistent in Wales, and it is arguable that the real change in poetic references to the Arthurian legend did not come until the fifteenth century. In the fourteenth century, Arthur's son Llachau continued to be mentioned as a standard of praise (by the poets Bleddyn Ddu and Rhisierdyn), Medrawd's name could still have a praiseworthy connotation (in a poem by Gwilym Ddu of Arfon) and Cai could still be cited for his *pwyll* ('wisdom') by Trahaearn Brydydd Mawr, and for his great strength by Hillyn. (On the portrayals of Medrawd and Cai, see chapter VIII.) Einion Offeiriad, in his praise of Sir Rhys ap Gruffudd (*c.* 1320), referred in quick succession to the traditional heroes of Arthur himself, Geraint, Gwalchmai and Peredur, in a manner which would have been at home a century earlier. When Dafydd ap Gwilym referred to Melwas's abduction of Gwenhwyfar, he was alluding to Welsh tradition, not to Continental stories of the queen's infidelity.

Reference to the full range of the Matter of Britain does not appear until even later, and only in the work of certain poets. Siôn ap Hywel, Siôn Ceri and Huw ap Dafydd ap Llywelyn ap Madog, in the later fifteenth century and the first half of the sixteenth, provide numerous allusions to the Arthurian figures of Geoffrey's HISTORY and international romance, while other poets failed to name a single Arthurian hero. Guto'r Glyn, in his praise of Siôn Hanmer (a gentleman of north Wales who flourished in the years 1461–8) compared him with the Nine Worthies, a Continental tradition which placed Arthur alongside other heroes such as Alexander, Caesar and Charlemagne. Medrawd's treachery, a central theme of international Arthurian legend from Geoffrey onwards, seems not to be mentioned by any Welsh poet until the work of Tudur Aled, again in the early sixteenth century. We may suppose that, increasingly through the later Middle Ages, poets and their audiences held a mixture of traditions and allusions in their minds, much as people today may discuss 'the Arthurian legend' without distinguishing (sometimes even being unaware of) the very various parts which made up the developed whole.

Another important poetic development of the fourteenth century and later is that Arthurian women, as well as men, began to be named by the poets. Apart from the single, indirect, reference to Gwenhwyfar by Hywel ab Owain, the women of the Arthurian legend are completely absent from the court poetry before 1282. Gwenhwyfar herself is not frequently mentioned even in the work of later poets (see chapter VIII); but Eigr (*Igerna*, Ygraine: Arthur's mother in Geoffrey's HISTORY and later), Luned, Enid and Esyllt all occur. This increase is partly due to the greater occurrence of women as subjects in the work of these later poets compared with their predecessors, and partly because Arthurian references and also references to ancient history (classical heroes) both became more frequent in the poetry composed after 1282, while non-Arthurian heroes from within Welsh literature received less attention. The Arthurian legend had taken its place in international literature, and perhaps was being cited as much in that capacity as for its Welsh roots.

If it is accepted that the Arthurian legend had its origins in local folklore in Wales, Cornwall and Brittany, then one important question arises: what effect did the international popularity of the developed legend have on the folklore itself in Wales? It is very difficult to judge how much feedback occurred. Apart from the wonders mentioned in the HISTORIA BRITTONUM, further pieces of local folklore appear in Wales and elsewhere, once there are records of a kind liable to show that sort of material. Two themes are consistently prominent: Arthur's household furniture (such as his attempted table in the Life of St Carannog, discussed earlier), and suggestions that Arthur was a giant (compare his reference to *men as vile as these* in RHONABWY), or at least had giant-like abilities. The two themes went together, inasmuch as the furniture was often of larger-than-life size. In the south-west (Devon or Cornwall) Arthur's seat and his oven were pointed out to travellers as early as 1113; the same account shows us Cornishmen in Bodmin holding vehemently the belief that Arthur would come again. In Scotland in the 1120s a circular sculpted building, probably of Roman construction, was known as 'Arthur's palace', and was claimed to show the warlike achievements of Arthur the soldier; a century later this building was known as 'Arthur's oven'. These 'ovens' referred to Arthur the huntsman: in the Irish countryside there are frequent examples of 'Fionn's cooking-place', because of that hero's enthusiasm for the chase. Later in the same century 'Arthur's bed-chamber' was known in the city of Carlisle, and we have already noted Gerald of Wales's reference to 'Arthur's seat' in the Brecon Beacons in the 1190s.

What is interesting about these references is that their nature does not alter as time goes on. In the thirteenth century, when Welsh poets might refer to Arthur the Emperor and Continental storytellers were preoccupied with the Holy Grail, a rock in Herefordshire was known as 'Arthur's stone'. Later names of rocks and antiquities elsewhere suggest that this was probably a reference to his gigantic strength: from the sixteenth century onwards, particularly in Wales and Cornwall, megalithic monuments are called 'Arthur's quoit' (*Coetan Arthur* in Wales), evidently because he would throw them for sport or as a special feat. ('Quoit' here means what is nowadays termed a 'discus'.) So common are the names Arthur's Quoit and The Giant's Quoit for cromlechs in Cornwall that 'quoit' has become a standard archaeological term for these megalithic monuments. In Brittany, a cromlech near Trébeurden was known as Arthur's grave. Bwrdd Arthur ('Arthur's table') is a hill fort on Anglesey situated at the eastern end of Traeth Coch, and called *Rounde Table* in 1562; and Arthur's Seat in Edinburgh is recorded in 1508. It is unknown how old these names are, but that is actually less important than the consistency and persistence of the habit: in one way, the more recent some examples are, the more impressive this phenomenon becomes.

A recent book on giant-lore in Wales provides numerous further examples of such names. Although the theme of Arthur's gigantic size and strength is scarcely articulated in medieval texts, it probably lies behind the ninth-century naming of Arthur's dog as Caball (*Cafall*, 'Horse'), and William of Malmesbury (1120s) mentioned the great size of Gawain's (Gwalchmai's) grave on the seashore. It may have been because Arthur and his men were so often portrayed tackling giants, as in CULHWCH and Geoffrey's HISTORY, that he was considered one himself.

Different Arthurian explanations for notable stones also occurred. As mentioned earlier, a large rock in Ruthin town (Denbighshire) is known as Maen Huail, because upon it Arthur beheaded Huail, a persistently provocative brother of St Gildas. The manner of his provocation portrayed the king in a decidedly undignified light. Arthur was dancing in woman's dress in order to approach a particular girl, but he limped from a wound which Huail had given him during a previous conflict over another girl; Huail identified the king and taunted him over his limp. This tale, recounted in the sixteenth century by Elis Gruffydd, is evidently related to the earlier one in the Life of St Gildas whereby Arthur slew Huail because of his raiding; there has been interchange between the oral and written traditions. Elis Gruffydd also reported a story from the Gloucester area that King Arthur and his warriors were asleep in a cave – perhaps the earliest explicit reference in Welsh to Arthur as a hero who will return.

Two examples of local names from Cornwall are worth mentioning, not because they are different but because they parallel what is found much more frequently in Wales, and also because of the interest in finding that such pieces of local folklore survived the decline and death of the language in that county.

In the bleak upland of Goss Moor, in central Cornwall, a large stone with hoof-shaped indentations, near to a Giant's Quoit megalith, was known as King Arthur's Stone in the eighteenth century, and a local antiquary reported that the imprints *were made by King Arthur's horse's feet, when he resided at Castle Denis* [a nearby hill-fort], *and hunted in the Goss-Moor.* The parallels of this account with the ninth-century Welsh story about Arthur's dog (called 'Horse') leaving its footprint in a stone while hunting the Twrch Trwyth are striking. This local tradition need not have been especially ancient in itself; what is important is its similarity to the ninth-century story, and the distance in time and space between the two accounts.

The parallel is explained more fully in the other Cornish item to be noted, recorded at the same period on Bodmin Moor in east Cornwall, where the Cornish language had probably been extinct for about five hundred years by the mid-eighteenth century. A hilltop rock, still known today as King Arthur's Bed (more furniture!), was reported by the antiquary William Borlase, who added that some rock basins nearby were known as Arthur's Troughs, in which he used to feed his dogs; and *whatever is great, and the use and author unknown, is attributed to Arthur.* Once again this folklore refers to Arthur the huntsman, feeding his hounds on the moorland. The writer's comment, that Arthur was invoked to explain major features of the landscape, neatly summarizes the consistent motivation behind these pieces of local lore, going back to the ninth-century HISTORIA BRITTONUM.

The question, therefore, arises as to how these more

recent names came to be given, and which aspect of Arthur they illustrate. The similarity of the two eighteenth-century Cornish examples to the ninth-century ones from the Welsh Marches need hardly be stressed. It is generally assumed that such folklore, when first recorded as late as the eighteenth century (or sometimes, in Wales, even in the nineteenth) is due to the literary legend. But it is not clear how that would have operated – why a local Welsh or Cornish farmer should name a rock Arthur's Bed or Arthur's Stone, in either the thirteenth century or the eighteenth, as a result of reading or hearing (say) Geoffrey's HISTORY, PEREDUR or Malory, or a story derived from these. Since we know that such names, and doubtless the stories that went with them, were already current in Cornwall, Wales and Scotland, before the international legend developed, it is simpler to suppose that what we find at later periods represents the continuation of the local folklore, largely unchanged: fresh instances of such names may have been produced at any time down to the recent past.

Of course, there has also been feedback from the literary legend. At Glastonbury, for example, there was a deliberate decision in about 1190 to discover Arthur's and Guinevere's graves. This was done partly for political reasons, to emphasize that Arthur was dead, and perhaps partly for financial ones, since Glastonbury Abbey was in need of money for rebuilding work. We have seen that Arthur was associated with Glastonbury in Welsh story (though not necessarily in local lore) rather earlier than that; but this event provides a good example of the conscious creation of local legend. It may well be that Arthur's international fame served to maintain or influence existing folklore elsewhere; for instance, references to Arthur as 'King' (as in the two Cornish examples) may be due to his literary representation; and at major sites, including Glastonbury or Tintagel, it would be impossible to distinguish local tradition from literary feedback; but the basic form of the local lore seems to have been so persistent that in many minor instances, such as the Cornish ones given above, it would be difficult to maintain any direct influence from the literary legend.

The conclusion of this analysis is that, although there must have been feedback from Arthur's literary representation into local traditions, nevertheless, when we find Arthur's name attached to natural features or ancient monuments, as it is all over Wales, we are witnessing examples of a phenomenon which goes back over a thousand years, largely unchanged, to the ninth-century HISTORIA BRITTONUM, and doubtless beyond that too. The attribution need not be anything like that old in any individual case, but the practice is demonstrably so.

VIII

Some Arthurian Characters

It has already been observed that the character of Arthur himself is rarely developed in any detail. His literary success through the ages has been partly due to the fact that he can be given any colouring according to the wishes of a particular writer – or of a particular literary fashion – by projecting a particular agenda onto the figure and its world. Writers following along these lines have not usually developed his character for its own sake. Arthur's accompanying warriors or knights have received more attention, from the time of CULHWCH and 'Pa ŵr yw'r porthor?' onwards. In this chapter a few well-known Arthurian characters will be examined, since they constitute such an important dimension of Arthur himself and of the development of his legend. Out of the many that could be chosen the first two, Cai and Bedwyr, are Arthur's most important companions in the earlier Welsh texts, while Medrawd, Gwenhwyfar and Gwalchmai came to prominence in the later international legend, though they have their roots in Welsh tradition.

Cai is the most important of Arthur's warriors in Welsh literature, and also the most complex; he is the only one who has himself been the subject of a modern scholarly study. From the poem 'Pa ŵr yw'r porthor?' onwards he has been celebrated as Arthur's chief companion; indeed, that poem (or rather the surviving fragment of it) has been described as 'really a glorification of Cai'. There is no evidence that Cai was originally an independent hero: from his earliest appearance, his role is always as Arthur's assistant – usually with Bedwyr as well, but Cai is always named first. It is Cai who shows the initiative when the pair tackle Dillus the Bearded in CULHWCH – and who, therefore, becomes the target of Arthur's mocking *englyn* for their cowardly method. After that episode Cai drops out of the story; but the author has previously given not one but two accounts of Cai's special abilities, one as prophesied by his father Cynyr within the list of Arthur's warriors (his physical coldness, especially of his hands, resolute nature, ability to make his burden invisible and to endure water and fire, and excellence as a retainer), the other shortly afterwards, when Cai begins the search for Olwen (his ability to survive under water or without sleep, to give unhealable wounds, to be taller than the trees – and his physical heat, especially of his hands!); and we also learn, again within the list of warriors, that Arthur eventually avenged Cai when he was slain, as if showing that there was no hard feeling on Arthur's part after Cai had abandoned him later in the tale.

In later romance, French and Welsh, Cai (Kei) is the outspoken, irritable knight who voices uncomfortable truths or unhelpful comments. There are suggestions of this role as early as CULHWCH, but it was developed in romance so that the portrayal of him became consistently sharp-tongued, whereas it had been mixed in earlier Welsh literature. We may note his outspoken comments in the three Welsh Romances (for example, his unfriendly reception of Peredur at Arthur's court, similar to his reluctance for the rules to be broken to admit Culhwch) – and, of course, in the corresponding passages in Chrétien's romances. Only in the late poem about Trystan and Esyllt does he appear in a kindly light (see p. 70).

Similarly, in Y SEINT GREAL Cai plays his part as in the French romances: in the first section it is Cai who reminds Arthur that he should not dine on a major feast day without some adventure first arriving at the court. In the second section he has a prominent role, killing Arthur's son Llachau and then bringing to Arthur's court the head of the giant whom Llachau has killed, claiming it as his own success – an episode developing from the earlier tradition of Cai's giant-killing exploits, but also similar to the wooing of Isolde in Gottfried of Strasburg's TRISTRANT (early thirteenth century), where the villainous steward claims to have killed the dragon by bringing its head to court, while Tristrant lies in a swoon. Subsequently, Cai in Y SEINT GREAL dwells in exile in Brittany and comes to ravage Arthur's realm during the king's absence; but (as in CULHWCH) Arthur does not become hostile towards him, showing no enthusiasm to avenge Llachau or punish Cai.

The negative portrayal of Cai in the romances contrasts notably with that found in Welsh court poetry (see below), but it seems to develop hints already present in CULHWCH, and may perhaps have been developed from Welsh tales now lost but current in the twelfth century. It is evident that his exile in Brittany may have developed from his departure from Arthur's court, as mentioned in CULHWCH, even though the reason for it is different.

Cai appears in two of the dialogue-poems – in that of

Melwas, where he is named in the third person as (we assume) Gwenhwyfar's standard of valour and strength, a comparison unfavourable to Melwas, and in that of Trystan, in an amicable exchange with Esyllt. These two texts seem to show the Cai of CULHWCH and 'Pa ŵr yw'r porthor?', rather than that of the Matter of Britain. In the court poetry the few references to Cai are notable for their positive aspect. He receives only one mention in the twelfth century, that by Cynddelw already quoted (p. 57), associating him with Dillus, and citing him for his strength; and one more mention in the thirteenth century, by Elidir Sais, again naming Cai and Bedwyr as military heroes. We have already seen (p. 100) how Trahaearn Brydydd Mawr, in the fourteenth century, cited *pwyll Cai* ('Cai's wisdom'), which still seems to ignore the image of the French romances; and the same is true of other references at this period, including two by Dafydd ap Gwilym to his *gwrol* ('heroic') nature and to his ability to overtop the trees.

In Welsh folklore Cai was, like Arthur, a giant; his epithet *Cai Hir* ('Cai the tall') bears this out, and a pass in Snowdonia had the name *Gwryd Cai* ('Cai's fathom, Cai's armspan') in the twelfth century; that place-name occurs twice elsewhere in medieval Wales. The early-modern poem, with accompanying explanation, in which Cai laments Dillus, his companion in hunting the fox of Arllechwedd, seems to continue the favourable image of Cai seen in the earlier poetry. It seems, then, that Cai succeeded in remaining an ambivalent character in Welsh literature, embracing admirable strength and valour as well as a prickly temper, despite his negative portrayal in romance literature.

Bedwyr is a simpler character, partly through being portrayed in less detail. He consistently appears as Arthur's staunchly reliable companion, from 'Pa ŵr yw'r porthor?' and CULHWCH through to late romance. Sir Bedevere's best-known role today is his place by Arthur's side after the final battle, returning the sword to the lake; the Middle English STANZAIC MORTE ARTHUR (fourteenth century) is the earliest text to portray him thus, but the role continues the idea of his reliability from earlier Welsh texts. In CULHWCH Bedwyr receives one short description, stressing his handsomeness and his fighting prowess. For the most part he is simply an assistant to Cai, until Cai's withdrawal from the story; after that he plays a useful role helping Arthur, holding Cafall in the hunt of the Twrch. In 'Pa ŵr yw'r porthor?' his part is similar, though his exploits, as far as they are specified, seem to be ordinary military ones. His grave was on Tryfan mountain in Snowdonia, according to the 'Stanzas of the Graves'; but other references to him in poetry are mostly uninformative comparisons concerning his valour in battle.

In the Matter of Britain Bedwyr receives less attention. He is named only once in the Early Version of the Triads, very honourably, being added at the end of no. 20, 'Three Battle-crowned Men (Tri Thaleith-yawc Cat) of the Island of Britain', as crowned even above the three named heroes (compare the additional mention of Arthur in no. 2, 'Three Generous Men'). Geoffrey of Monmouth kept both him and Cai in much the same roles that they already had in Welsh literature: Beduerus is Arthur's cup-bearer, and the two of them assist Arthur in attacking the giant of Mont St Michel during the Continental campaign; Arthur rewards them with French ducal estates. Bedwyr's role in later romance dwindles. He is named only once, in passing, in the three Welsh Romances (in the list of Arthur's knights in GERAINT), and likewise in Chrétien's corresponding romances, with the same passing reference in EREC; and he is absent from both parts of Y SEINT GREAL. However, he retained his honourable position, to re-emerge in later literature in his place by Arthur's side.

The portrayal of Medrawd altered even more than that of Cai as the Arthurian legend developed. Although he was named in the Annals as having died at Camlan along with Arthur, he is absent from other early Welsh texts, conspicuously so in CULHWCH. Meilyr Brydydd, in his lament for the death of Gruffudd ap Cynan (died 1137), described Gruffudd as having *eissor Medrawd* ('the nature of Medrawd'), in a context which indicates that this meant valour in battle; and Meilyr's son Gwalchmai praised Madog ap Maredudd, king of Powys (died 1160) for having *Arthur gedernyd, menwyd Medrawd* ('Arthur's strength, the good nature of Medrawd'), evidently seeing no incongruity in mentioning them thus side by side. Two poets, Cynddelw and Gwynfardd Brycheiniog, used Medrawd as a standard of comparison, presumably of valour, to the Lord Rhys, king of South Wales (died 1197). Clearly the name Medrawd carried very different resonances from those which the name Modred carried later on.

The change was probably due to Geoffrey of Monmouth, who first narrated, and may well have invented, Modred's treachery in seizing both the crown and the queen while Arthur was campaigning on the Continent. It may be that Geoffrey based this episode partly on the earlier Welsh tale of the abduction of Gwenhwyfar by Melwas, replacing Melwas with Modred. Geoffrey's form of Modred's name is Cornish or Breton, not Welsh: in both regions the form *Modröd* or *Modred* was in use as a personal name in the ninth or tenth century, and that form is likely to have been the original one; the Welsh form *Medrawd* then shows reinterpretation, perhaps by analogy with *medru* ('to be able, to aim, shoot, hit'). Geoffrey's use of the non-Welsh form carries implications concerning his sources, of course, but that need not concern us here. The occurrence of *Modred* as an ordinary personal name in Cornwall and Brittany shows that the name lacked evil connotations there, as it evidently did in Wales, as shown by the court poetry. In Cornwall the name survived beyond the Norman Conquest, almost uniquely among Celtic personal names in that region, and it occurs as a surname as late as the fourteenth century. But Geoffrey's story meant that in romance Modred's name became a byword for treachery.

If it is correct to deduce that Geoffrey imposed the story of treachery upon a previously esteemed character, then the court poets apparently ignored the new development, and succeeded in doing so for a remarkably long time. Medrawd appears neutrally in the fifteenth-century 'Twenty-four Knights' Triads, with no mention of his treachery; and the earliest poetic mention of his conflict with Arthur seems to be in the work of Tudur Aled (early sixteenth century). Although this poetic resistance was presumably due to the strength of the pre-Geoffrey tradition about him, its longevity is nevertheless impressive, especially given that the later Triads contain several allusions to Medrawd,

Gwenhwyfar and Camlan, clearly linking them in a causal manner.

It is difficult, because of the lack of early material, to know how much the reputation of Gwenhwyfar altered over the centuries. Although she is mentioned in CULHWCH, no allusions to any stories are made there: she is the last of Arthur's possessions which he excludes from his offer to Culhwch; two sons of hers (not said to be Arthur's!) are named; and in the list of the ladies of Arthur's court she receives the title *Penn Rianed yr Ynys Honn* ('chief of the ladies of this island', reflecting Arthur's own title), and also a sister, Gwenhwyach, probably another wordplaying fancy of the author. She appears in Geoffrey's HISTORY, of course. Her attitude to Modred's usurpation is not made clear there, although Geoffrey's claimed 'restraint' in narrating the episode hints that it was even more scandalous than he chose to say; that could imply enthusiasm on the queen's part.

Gwenhwyfar's name is absent from the Early Version of the Triads, and from the poetry until the fourteenth century, except for Hywel ab Owain's mention of the 'fair lady' at Ogrfan's court, which probably alludes to her (see pp. 56–7). Even Dafydd ap Gwilym, while clearly referring to Melwas's abduction of Gwenhwyfar, names her only as *ferch Ogfran Gawr* ('the daughter of Ogfran the giant'). However, he does name her in another poem (*rwyf Gwenhwyfar* ('Gwenhwyfar's pride') – in a context suggestive of adultery), perhaps her earliest named appearance in Welsh poetry, except for her 'Dialogue' with Melwas, if that is earlier. Women called Gwenhwyfar occurred in Wales during the later

Middle Ages in north Wales (apparently few in the south), so the resonances of her name cannot have been too scandalous at that date: Gwenhwyfar, the wife of Hywel ap Tudur ap Gruffudd of Coedan (Anglesey), was praised in elegies by both Gronw Gyriog and Mab Clochyddyn in the fourteenth century.

Judging by the few prose references to Gwenhwyfar in Welsh before 1200, and her absence from the early court poetry, it seems unlikely that she would be well known today if it had not been for the major role which her adultery played in Continental romance. The popular rhyme quoted by Rhys in 1891,

> Gwenhwyfar ferch Ogrfan Gawr,
> drwg yn fechan, gwaeth yn fawr
>
> (Gwenhwyfar daughter of Ogrfan the giant,
> bad when little, worse when big)

presumably alludes to this misbehaviour, and the later Triads provide evidence for the knowledge of it in later medieval Wales; but her reputation is due largely to Geoffrey and later, non-Welsh, romances. Her earliest major parts in extant Welsh literature, therefore, occur in the translations of Geoffrey's HISTORY, establishing the association between her, Medrawd and Camlan, and in the second part of Y SEINT GREAL, where her adulterous reputation is mentioned several times – as Arthur is himself informed by a maiden who fails to recognize him:

Eissyoes ny daw ef yr rawc o Gaer Llion, rac ovyn mynet ereill a'e wreic, heruyd ual y kiglefi dywedut amdanunt.

116

(Nevertheless he [Arthur] *will not ever come away from Caerleon, for fear of others going with his wife, as I have heard tell about them.)*

Although there was clearly a legend about Gwen-hwyfar's abduction independently of Geoffrey's HISTORY, that legend seems to have been eclipsed by his development of it; in Wales the eclipse probably occurred in the fourteenth century, when we have both Dafydd's reference to Melwas and the un-flattering reference to her in Y SEINT GREAL.

Two fourteenth-century texts of the Welsh Laws specify that a song performed privately to the queen in her chamber should be about Camlan: by that date, a reference to Camlan would doubtless have car-ried connotations of Medrawd and Gwenhwyfar's adultery, so the song would have acted as a warning to the queen of the consequences of misbehaving.

Gwalchmai, Arthur's nephew, is similarly difficult to chart, since the early mentions of him are so few. He occurs as Arthur's nephew both in CULHWCH (where he plays little part) and in William of Malmesbury's 'Deeds of the Kings of England', which describes the discovery of his giant-sized grave, fourteen feet long, upon the seashore in south Wales. The mid-twelfth-century poet Gwalchmai ap Meilyr must have been born before the completion of Geoffrey's HISTORY, where *Gualguanus* (Gawain) plays a valiant military role: if the poet was named after the Arthurian character, as seems likely, then Gwalch-mai's reputation for fine speech must date from before Geoffrey. (Gwalchmai the poet did not, how-ever, specialize in Arthurian allusions: his only surviving one is that to *Arthur's strength, Medrawd's good nature*, mentioned earlier.) Gwalchmai appears in one early Triad, *Tri Deifnyawc* ('Three Endowed Men', no. 4), where he is named along with Llachau son of Arthur; *deifnyawc* ('richly endowed') is assumed to signify entitlement by inheritance. Gwalchmai was used as an honourable comparison by Cynddelw in the twelfth century, *taerualch ual Gwalchmei* ('fervently strong like Gwalchmai'), of Owain Gwynedd, died 1170, and by Y Prydydd Bychan and Einion Wan in the thirteenth.

Gwalchmai's main claim to fame is as a hero of later romance (Gawain in English). The three Welsh Romances contain the Continental image of him as a model of courtesy: in both GERAINT and PEREDUR he succeeds where Cai has failed to persuade the estranged hero to return to Arthur's court. (So also, once again, in the corresponding passages in Chrétien's romances.) This is the reason for his epithet in later Welsh literature, *tafod aur* ('golden-tongue', for example in the 'Twenty-four Knights of Arthur's Court'), and he fulfils that role again in the *englyn*-dialogue with Trystan.

What we seem to see overall in the treatment of these Arthurian heroes in later medieval Welsh literature is an apparent inconsistency between poetry and prose. Their portrayal in prose tended to reflect closely the developments in Continental romance, while poets continued the older Welsh traditions for much longer, insofar as there was a discrepancy between the two. Thus Cai and, more remarkably, Medrawd both remained honourable and valiant in poetry; and Gwenhwyfar, as far as we can tell, remained a victim of abduction by Melwas, rather than a willing partner in adultery with Medrawd.

The likeliest explanation for this apparent inconsistency between prose and poetry is generally felt to be that the poets were selective in how many of the Continental developments they chose to adopt. Their selectivity appears to be at variance with their adoption of an imperial role for Arthur, which the poets did embrace from the time of Prydydd y Moch (late twelfth century) onwards, and perhaps earlier too, depending on the date of the *englynion* concerning Geraint, where Arthur receives the epithet *amherawdyr*.

The greatest consciousness of inconsistency between the older and newer traditions would have been in the case of Medrawd; the problem of how to deal with his betrayal of Arthur would depend partly upon how Arthur himself was viewed, and to that we now turn, in conclusion.

IX

Was There an Arthur of the Welsh?

Two related questions remain to be considered. First, was there a fully developed Arthurian legend in Wales, or only a range of independent tales and local folklore? Second, in what sense was there actually an 'Arthur of the Welsh' in the Middle Ages? These questions are worth discussing, even if definite answers cannot be provided. They form contributory parts of a larger question: what was the exact nature of the Arthurian legend in Wales before Geoffrey of Monmouth altered it for ever?

Whether there was a fully developed Arthurian legend in Wales, as is provided by Geoffrey in recounting his birth, achievements and death, must remain a matter of opinion; but we may ask why we should suppose that there was. The pieces of Arthurian lore which survive from before Geoffrey's time – such as the local tales from the Welsh Marches, the oven and chair in south-west England (probably with local stories, now lost, to explain them) and the stories incorporated into CULHWCH – are probably the most authentic type of Arthurian material to survive. Such stories do not need a wider framework: they can be complete in themselves, just as CULHWCH itself is. As in a television series which recounts each week a fresh adventure for a particular hero, that hero's birth and death may not need to be narrated. Such amplifications might come later, either in the form of fresh local episodes (the death of Fionn was located at notable points in the Irish landscape) or perhaps at a learned, written stage of the legend, maybe when it was fitted into historical frameworks. There was evidently a well-known story about Arthur's death at Camlan in existence before 1100, as reflected in the Annals and CULHWCH; but Geoffrey was the first to name Arthur's father as Uther Pendragon. ('Uthr' does appear fleetingly in Welsh texts which may be earlier, though not in a paternal role except in 'Arthur and the Eagle' which is of uncertain date.) It was also Geoffrey who gave the earliest account of Arthur's conception at Tintagel.

Of course, our sources at this early date are undoubtedly deficient, despite the overview which CULHWCH and 'Pa ŵr yw'r porthor?' provide through their allusions to other tales; but the nature of the surviving material makes it reasonable to doubt whether there need have been a complete, rounded 'Arthurian legend' in Wales before the twelfth century. It may be closer to the truth to envisage a multiplicity of individual stories, which might have included Arthur's death, or at least his final battle, and maybe his conception or birth as well.

As for the second question – was there an Arthur of the Welsh? – in one sense the answer is an immediate and obvious 'Yes'. Wales, Cornwall and Brittany all had a strong tradition of Arthurian lore, well before Geoffrey of Monmouth gave to the legend the momentum which has ensured its international popularity down to the present day. It was undoubtedly from Welsh sources, probably also from Cornish and possibly from Breton ones, that Geoffrey drew much of the inspiration for his portrayal of Arthur in his

HISTORY, even though his imagination also made a major contribution.

However, the question remains of whether there was a distinctively Welsh portrayal of Arthur, and, if so, to what extent that survived his international literary success. Furthermore, the sources before Geoffrey's time are few and perhaps partial: what can be concluded with confidence about the way in which Welsh audiences viewed the figure of Arthur before Geoffrey altered its image for ever? Unfortunately, we cannot know whether there was a distinctively Welsh portrayal of Arthur, because of the lack of full information about his image in Cornwall and Brittany at the same period. The fullest information for those two regions comes from the journey of the Laon canons through Cornwall in 1113, and from that we learn of the local furniture, comparable with later lore in Wales, and also of Arthur's role as promised deliverer in both Cornwall and Brittany, raising strong national feeling when he was mocked by outsiders. What follows concerning the figure of Arthur in Wales may have applied equally, or partially, in those other regions as well.

The suggestion offered here is that certain assumptions have been made too readily about the figure of Arthur in the earliest Welsh sources, partly through the uncritical use of words such as 'heroic', and partly owing to uncertainty, which still exists, over how to approach certain crucial literary sources such as CULHWCH, RHONABWY and the saints' Lives. There is a danger of reading these texts too subtly, combing them for every last clue to ancient traditions, instead of reading them as the works of authors who were putting their own interpretation upon the material, and perhaps intended them light-heartedly for the most part, though with very various aims.

It is worth considering the idea that Arthur was often an intrinsically comic character, and that Arthurian tales, within the range of literary and storytelling material available in medieval Wales, occupied a humorous role, perhaps approximately comparable with comic-strip literature today. A few items which may argue against this idea will be examined shortly, but first the points in its favour. Arthur's portrayal as a giant, of which there are hints from the very earliest sources (his dog named 'Horse' in the ninth-century Wonders; his nephew's outsize grave in the 1120s), and which has remained so consistent down to the most recent folklore, is one such point. Giants are often portrayed as undignified figures (as well as terrifying at the same time) – opponents who, when malevolent, cannot be overpowered so must be outwitted, and who are, therefore, necessarily slow-minded. In the case of Arthur, however, this would be qualified as slow-minded but essentially good-natured, comparable with Obélix in the Astérix cartoons, or Desperate Dan in boys' comics, rather than Goliath or the Cyclops.

Several works make good sense when read in this light. The dialogue of 'Arthur and the Eagle' seems to require such an image, with some of Arthur's questions turning the eagle into a paragon of didactic patience. (The most obvious instance is Arthur's hope of storming heaven in order to rescue his dead nephew, followed by his assumption that if he himself could not do it, perhaps somebody else could.) It would explain Arthur's selection for the role of slow-witted but well-intentioned questioner in this poem if he was often envisaged in such a light. It is also arguable that the saints' Lives make better sense when so read, with Arthur as well-meaning but slow-witted and capricious, instead of portraying a negative, hostile side of the leader as has often been assumed. Once again, the danger of misinterpretation may arise from reading the sources too seriously: didactic works, including saints' Lives, are quite capable of embracing a comical element.

The poem 'Pa ŵr yw'r porthor?' may also be illuminated by such an interpretation of Arthur: his nostalgic propensity to ramble on about his warriors' achievements would then cause him to lose track of the purpose of his answer. Dignity was not one of Arthur's attributes in Welsh, until his imperial status in Geoffrey's HISTORY and sub-sequently the Three Romances thrust it upon him. The tales of CULHWCH and RHONABWY must both be read as humorous pieces, albeit of very different kinds: CULHWCH as a wild romp of exuberance, RHONABWY as a parody or satire, maybe with a serious edge to it as well, were we able to identify that with assurance.

This interpretation would also mean that there was no conflict or discrepancy between the portrayal of Arthur in CULHWCH and that in the saints' Lives, as is sometimes supposed: if the latter works were partly humorous, then they could be read in a manner compatible with the vernacular tale. It might also be argued that the portrayal of Arthur in OWAIN, though largely following the developed, Continental image of Arthur the emperor as found in Chrétien's work, contains one or two touches of this earlier, undignified, Arthur, falling asleep during the pre-dinner drinks at court. But, for the most part, the older portrayal necessarily disappeared from Welsh literature once Arthur's international career was launched.

However, there are some pieces of early Welsh literature which do not fit well with this inter-pretation. The story of Arthur killing his own son, in the ninth-century Wonders of Britain, must surely have been a tragic tale. The disastrous overseas expedition in 'Preiddiau Annwn' is portrayed by the legendary Taliesin as a solemn affair; this no doubt served the poet's own literary ends, but the fact that the tale could be so used suggests that it already had a serious aspect. Moreover, when the twelfth-century court poets, and earlier the GODODDIN, cited Arthur as a standard of military valour or generosity, they are unlikely to have been comparing their patrons and heroes to a figure of fun. Such similes drew rather upon Arthur the military defender of Britain, as in the HISTORIA BRITTONUM. Finally, Arthur's role as promised deliverer seems to fit poorly with a comical figure, for that is inherently a serious role. However, the anger of Cornishmen when Arthur was ridiculed by the visiting French canons may work either way: offence can particu-larly be caused when those objects reserved for affec-tionate humour within a community are mocked by uncomprehending outsiders.

However, even these serious aspects are not wholly incompatible with the idea of Arthur as an inher-ently undignified figure. We can suppose, first, that this indignity was only one aspect of his portrayal, and that he could fill other roles as well; even comic strips may at times consider serious issues of destiny or morality, and a comical figure may carry all the more weight when suddenly cast in a serious or tragic role. Moreover, among the court poets Prydydd y Moch, in the late twelfth century, seems to have been the first to embrace the idea of Arthur as a dignified emperor, as far as the extant material shows. Before his time there are only three references to Arthur in that type of poetry: the allusions to Arthur's strength and to the din of his warband are compatible with the giant image, and only the reference to his *lluch ryfig* ('lightning confidence') might be at odds with it (see p. 52). Similarly, the GODODDIN reference could have been an allusion to Arthur as a legendary giant, such that even Gwawrddur could not hope to match him in might or military achievement. The force of the comparisons would indeed be weakened if Arthur was solely a comical figure; but if that was merely one aspect of his gigantic strength then it need not have impaired his value as a paragon of strength and valour. The poet Gwalchmai ap Meilyr saw fit to attribute *bar Golias* ('the ferocity of Goliath') to his patron, Owain Gwynedd, so it is evident that our own ideas of what was complimentary are not necessarily a reliable guide to the ideas of the court poets or their patrons.

It could also be argued that this image of Arthur would be insufficient to explain Geoffrey of Monmouth's development of the figure. If Arthur was primarily an undignified giant, why should Geoffrey have become so preoccupied by him as to have been nicknamed after him ('Geoffrey Arthur'), and to have selected him to develop into his international warlord? Again, it would have been other aspects of the legend that Geoffrey knew or chose to admire –

Arthur's military achievements against the English, rather than his conquests of supernatural monsters. Indeed, the slightly derogatory, or admiringly sceptical, comments of other non-Welsh writers in the twelfth century (William of Malmesbury, William of Newburgh) seem to relate more closely to the military leader (albeit with some legendary element, as in the Twelve Battles or the unknown grave) than to the slow-witted giant. Perhaps the undignified Arthur was emphasized more in oral narrative (reflected indirectly in literary derivatives, such as CULHWCH and, seemingly, the saints' Lives), while certain written or formal compositions, including court poetry, preferred to emphasize the military leader; but elements of both could be present simultaneously. Writers outside Wales, such as William of Malmesbury, would perhaps have learned about Arthur predominantly from more formal sources, and thus have known more about the military leader; but if they also heard rumours of the more imaginative local tales, such as William had evidently heard about Gawain, that would explain their scepticism about Arthur. At times the portrayal of Arthur may even have bordered upon the heroic, in the more precise sense of that word preferred here (that is, within the code of behaviour identifiable in a work such as the GODODDIN); but the material does not enable us to assert that with assurance.

This multifaceted image of Arthur can be better understood by turning to the portrayal of Fionn in early Irish literature, where the quantity of material is so much greater. There we see Fionn as honoured defender of the island, and Fionn in tragic roles (notably in the feud against his nephew Diarmaid for the love of Gráinne); but some early short tales (such as 'Fionn and the Man in the Tree') have a comical and undignified element to them as well. Like Arthur and Cai, Fionn and his warriors are often portrayed as giants, though it is unclear whether the theme can be traced earlier than the twelfth-century ACALLAM NA SENÓRACH, where their huge size, along with the great size of their dogs, is emphasized at the beginning of the work. The greater quantity of material available for the Irish hero makes it clear that different roles, including comical ones, can perfectly well be found applied to heroes who are sometimes cast in serious, honourable and even tragic roles.

It is possible, too, that Arthur was not necessarily a figure with whom the audience was expected to engage with a great deal of sympathy. We are used to an Arthur who stands for a noble ideal, even if he is himself flawed in living up to it; but in some types of story, particularly humorous ones, the 'hero' may be the object of unfortunate incidents without necessarily attracting our sympathy. It is even possible that the abduction of Arthur's queen had a comical element to begin with; there may be surviving hints of that in the 'Dialogue of Melwas and Gwenhwyfar', and in the lack of sympathy for Arthur's plight in the Melwas episode of the Life of St Gildas, although the focus there is of course on the saint. Any such comic element was removed by Geoffrey among the other alterations that he made to this story, and Arthur became thereafter a tragic figure; but Medrawd's continued appearance as a favourable comparison in Welsh poetry might have been facilitated if Arthur himself, in the earlier Welsh tradition, was not a character with whom the audience was particularly required to sympathize.

The possibility cannot be pressed; but, again, it is worth bearing in mind as a potential background for the reception which Geoffrey's 'new' story might have found in Wales.

It is evidently untenable to argue that Arthur invariably had an undignified, slow-witted side to his character. But it may be useful to bear in mind the possibility of such an aspect, so as to broaden our understanding of some of the roles in which he was cast in early Welsh literature, and as a background for some others. Whether or not that is accepted, it is clear that the figure of Arthur in the earliest Welsh literature can only be understood when the nature of each text in which he features is fully grasped, and that will continue to be the main focus of scholarly enquiry.

Select Bibliography

A full bibliography of the Arthurian legend would fill volumes. Reference is here restricted to basic texts, and to recent secondary works which will lead the reader on to further references, or to works which the author has found particularly useful for this book.

Chapter I: Introduction (pp. 1–2)

Bromwich, Rachel (ed.), TRIOEDD YNYS PRYDEIN. THE WELSH TRIADS, 2nd edn, Cardiff: University of Wales Press, 1978.

Bromwich, Rachel, A. O. H. Jarman, and Brynley F. Roberts (eds.), THE ARTHUR OF THE WELSH, Cardiff: University of Wales Press, 1991.

Chambers, E. K., ARTHUR OF BRITAIN, 2nd edn, Cambridge: Speculum Historiale, 1964.

Coe, J. B., and S. Young, THE CELTIC SOURCES FOR THE ARTHURIAN LEGEND, Felinfach: Llanerch, 1995.

Jones, Gwyn, and Thomas Jones (trans.), THE MABINOGION, London: Dent, 1949 and subsequent editions; and Jeffrey Gantz (trans.), THE MABINOGION, Harmondsworth: Penguin, 1976.

Jones, Thomas, 'Datblygiadau cynnar chwedl Arthur', BULLETIN OF THE BOARD OF CELTIC STUDIES, 17 (1956–8), 235–52; translated by Gerald Morgan as

'The early evolution of the legend of Arthur', NOTTINGHAM MEDIAEVAL STUDIES, 8 (1964), 3–21.

Padel, O. J., 'The nature of Arthur', CAMBRIAN MEDIEVAL CELTIC STUDIES, 27 (Summer 1994), 1–31.

Chapter II: The Earliest Texts (pp. 3–13)

Charles-Edwards, T., 'The Arthur of history', in Bromwich et al. (eds.), THE ARTHUR OF THE WELSH, op. cit.

Dumville, D. N., '*Historia Brittonum*: an Insular history from the Carolingian Age', in Anton Scharer and Georg Scheibelreiter (eds.), HISTORIOGRAPHIE IM FRÜHEN MITTELALTER, Wien: R. Oldenbourg, 1994, 406–34.

Jackson, K. H. (trans.), THE GODODDIN: THE OLDEST SCOTTISH POEM, Edinburgh: University Press, 1969.

Jarman, A. O. H. (ed. and trans.), ANEIRIN: THE GODODDIN, Llandysul: Gomer Press, 1988.

Morris, John (ed. and trans.), NENNIUS, BRITISH HISTORY AND THE WELSH ANNALS, Chichester: Phillimore, 1980.

Chapter III: Arthur's World: CULHWCH *and* 'Pa ŵr yw'r porthor?' *(pp. 14–33)*

Bromwich, Rachel, and D. Simon Evans (eds.), CULHWCH AND OLWEN: AN EDITION AND STUDY OF THE OLDEST ARTHURIAN TALE, Cardiff: University of Wales Press, 1992.

Child, Francis James, THE ENGLISH AND SCOTTISH POPULAR BALLADS, 5 vols., Boston: Houghton, Mifflin, 1882–98, I, no. 30 ('King Arthur and King Cornwall').

Edel, D., 'The Arthur of *Culhwch ac Olwen* as a figure

of epic-heroic tradition', READING MEDIEVAL STUDIES, 9 (1983), 3–15.

Ford, P. K., 'On the significance of some Arthurian names in Welsh', BULLETIN OF THE BOARD OF CELTIC STUDIES, 30 (1983), 268–73.

Haycock, M., ' "Some talk of Alexander and some of Hercules": three early medieval poems from the Book of Taliesin', CAMBRIDGE MEDIEVAL CELTIC STUDIES, 13 (Summer 1987), 7–38.

Padel, O. J., 'Some south-western sites with Arthurian associations', in Bromwich et al. (eds.), THE ARTHUR OF THE WELSH, op. cit.

Radner, J., 'Interpreting medieval irony: the case of *Culhwch ac Olwen*', CAMBRIDGE MEDIEVAL CELTIC STUDIES, 16 (Winter 1988), 41–60.

Roberts, B. F., '*Culhwch ac Olwen*, the Triads, saints' Lives', in Bromwich et al. (eds.), THE ARTHUR OF THE WELSH, op. cit.

Sims-Williams, P., 'The early Welsh Arthurian poems', in Bromwich et al. (eds.), THE ARTHUR OF THE WELSH, op. cit.

Chapter IV: Other Texts of the Central Middle Ages (pp. 34–63)

Bullock-Davies, Constance, '*Exspectare Arturum*: Arthur and the Messianic hope', BULLETIN OF THE BOARD OF CELTIC STUDIES, 29 (1980–1), 432–40.

Gerald of Wales, THE JOURNEY THROUGH WALES AND THE DESCRIPTION OF WALES, trans. Lewis Thorpe, Harmondsworth: Penguin, 1978.

Gruffudd, R. Geraint (general editor), CYFRES BEIRDD Y TYWYSOGION, 7 vols., Cardiff: University of Wales Press, 1991–6.

Haycock, Marged, ' "Preiddeu Annwn" and the figure of Taliesin', STUDIA CELTICA, 18–19 (1983–4), 52–78.

Henken, E., TRADITIONS OF THE WELSH SAINTS, Cambridge: D. S. Brewer, 1987.

Jones, T., 'The Black Book of Carmarthen "Stanzas of the Graves" ', PROCEEDINGS OF THE BRITISH ACADEMY, 53 (1967), 97–137.

Parry Owen, A., 'Mynegai i enwau priod ym marddoniaeth Beirdd y Tywysogion', LLÊN CYMRU, 20 (1997), 25–45.

Roberts, Brynley, 'Rhai o gerddi ymddiddan yn Llyfr Du Caerfyrddin', in Rachel Bromwich and R. Brinley Jones (eds.), ASTUDIAETHAU AR YR HENGERDD, STUDIES IN OLD WELSH POETRY, CYFLWYNEDIG I SYR IDRIS FOSTER, Cardiff: University of Wales Press, 1978, 281–325 (GERAINT, 'Pa ŵr yw'r porthor?' and GWYDDNAU).

Rowland, J., EARLY WELSH SAGA POETRY, Cambridge: D. S. Brewer, 1990, 240–7 (the *englynion* on Geraint ab Erbin).

Wade-Evans, A. W. (ed.), VITAE SANCTORUM BRITANNIAE ET GENEALOGIAE, Cardiff: University of Wales Press, 1944.

Chapter V: Three Dialogue Poems (pp. 64–71)

Coe, J. B., and S. Young, THE CELTIC SOURCES FOR THE ARTHURIAN LEGEND, op. cit., 103–15 ('Arthur and the Eagle'; 'Melwas and Gwenhwyfar').

Cross, T. P., 'A Welsh Tristan episode', STUDIES IN PHILOLOGY, 17 (1920), 93–110.

Haycock, M., BLODEUGERDD BARDDAS O GANU CREFYDDOL CYNNAR, Abertawe: Barddas, 1994, 297–312 ('Arthur and the Eagle').

Jones, Evan D., 'Melwas, Gwenhwyfar, a Chai', BULLETIN OF THE BOARD OF CELTIC STUDIES, 8 (1935–7), 203–8.

Parry-Williams, T. H. (ed.), CANU RHYDD CYNNAR, Caerdydd: Gwasg Prifysgol Cymru, 1932, no. 70 ('Ymddiddan rhwng Mair Fadlen a'r Creiriwr').

Rowland, J., EARLY WELSH SAGA POETRY, op. cit., 249–60 and 285–6.

Chapter VI: The Matter of Britain (pp. 72–93)

Bromwich, Rachel (ed.), TRIOEDD YNYS PRYDEIN, op. cit.

Davies, J. H., 'A Welsh version of the birth of Arthur', Y CYMMRODOR, 24 (1913), 247–64.

Geoffrey of Monmouth, THE HISTORY OF THE KINGS OF BRITAIN, trans. Lewis Thorpe, Harmondsworth: Penguin, 1966, and subsequent editions.

Goetinck, G. W. (ed.), HISTORIA PEREDUR VAB EFRAWC, Caerdydd: Gwasg Prifysgol Cymru, 1976.

Jones, Thomas (ed.), YSTORYAEU SEINT GREAL, part I, Y KEIS, Caerdydd: Gwasg Prifysgol Cymru, 1992.

Lewis, Henry (ed.), BRUT DINGESTOW, Caerdydd: Gwasg Prifysgol Cymru, 1942.

Lloyd-Morgan, C., 'Perceval in Wales: late medieval Welsh Grail traditions', in A. Adams, A. H. Diverres, K. Stern and K. Varty (eds.), THE CHANGING FACE OF ARTHURIAN ROMANCE: ESSAYS ON ARTHURIAN PROSE

ROMANCES IN MEMORY OF CEDRIC E. PICKFORD, Cambridge: D. S. Brewer, 1986, 78–91.

Padel, O. J., 'Geoffrey of Monmouth and Cornwall', CAMBRIDGE MEDIEVAL CELTIC STUDIES, 8 (Winter 1984), 1–28.

Roberts, Brynley (ed.), BRUT Y BRENHINEDD, LLAN-STEPHAN MS. 1 VERSION. SELECTIONS, Dublin: Institute for Advanced Studies, 1971.

Roberts, B. F., 'Geoffrey of Monmouth, *Historia Regum Britanniae* and *Brut y Brenhinedd*', in Bromwich et al. (eds.), THE ARTHUR OF THE WELSH, op. cit.

Roberts, B. F., STUDIES ON MIDDLE WELSH LITERATURE, Lampeter: Edwin Mellen, 1992.

Tatlock, J. S. P., THE LEGENDARY HISTORY OF BRITAIN, Berkeley and Los Angeles: University of California Press, 1950.

Thomson, R. L. (ed.), OWEIN OR CHWEDYL IARLLES Y FFYNNAWN, Dublin: Institute for Advanced Studies, 1968.

Thomson, R. L. (ed.), YSTORIA GEREINT UAB ERBIN, Dublin: Institute for Advanced Studies, 1997.

Williams, Robert (ed. and trans.), SELECTIONS FROM THE HENGWRT MSS., vol. I, Y SEINT GREAL, London: the editor, 1874–6.

Wright, Neil (ed.), THE HISTORIA REGUM BRITANNIAE OF GEOFFREY OF MONMOUTH: A SINGLE-MANUSCRIPT EDITION FROM BERN, BURGERBIBLIOTHEK, MS. 568, Cambridge: D. S. Brewer, 1984.

Chapter VII: The Continuing Tradition (pp. 94–107)

Andrews, Rhian M. et al. (eds.), CYFRES BEIRDD Y
TYWYSOGION, vol. 7, GWAITH BLEDDYN FARDD A BEIRDD
ERAILL AIL HANNER Y DRYDEDD GANRIF AR DDEG,
Caerdydd: Gwasg Prifysgol Cymru, 1996.

Fulton, Helen, 'Cyd-destun gwleidyddol *Breudwyt
Ronabwy*', LLÊN CYMRU, 22 (1999), 42–56.

Grooms, Chris, THE GIANTS OF WALES. CEWRI CYMRU,
Lampeter: Edwin Mellen, 1993.

Jones, D. Gwenallt (ed.), YR AREITHIAU PROS,
Caerdydd: Gwasg Prifysgol Cymru, 1934, 12–17 and
84–92 (ARAITH IOLO GOCH).

Jones, Thomas, 'A sixteenth-century version of the
Arthurian Cave legend', in M. Brahmer, S.
Helsztyński and J. Krzyżanowski (eds.), STUDIES IN
LANGUAGE AND LITERATURE IN HONOUR OF MARGARET
SCHLAUCH, Warszawa: PWN – Polish Scientific
Publishers, 1966, 175–85.

Jones, Thomas 'Chwedl Huail ap Caw ac Arthur', in
Jones, Thomas (ed.), ASTUDIAETHAU AMRYWIOL A
GYFLWYNIR I SYR THOMAS PARRY-WILLIAMS, Caerdydd:
Gwasg Prifysgol Cymru, 1968, 48–66.

Lloyd-Morgan, C., '*Breuddwyd Rhonabwy* and later
Arthurian literature', in Bromwich et al. (eds.), THE
ARTHUR OF THE WELSH, op. cit.

Padel, O. J., 'The nature of Arthur', op. cit.

Parry Owen, Ann (general editor), CYFRES BEIRDD YR
UCHELWYR, 14 vols. to date, Aberystwyth: Centre for
Advanced Welsh and Celtic Studies, 1994–.

Richards, Melville (ed.), BREUDWYT RONABWY,
Caerdydd: Gwasg Prifysgol Cymru, 1948.

Slotkin, E. M., 'The fabula, story and text of *Breuddwyd Rhonabwy*', CAMBRIDGE MEDIEVAL CELTIC STUDIES, 18 (Winter 1989), 89–111.

Tatlock, J. S. P., 'The English journey of the Laon canons', SPECULUM, 8 (1933), 454–65.

Chapter VIII: Some Arthurian Characters (pp. 108–19)

Bromwich, Rachel (ed.), TRIOEDD YNYS PRYDEIN, op. cit.

Gowans, Linda M., CEI AND THE ARTHURIAN LEGEND, Cambridge: D. S. Brewer, 1988.

Richards, Melville, 'Arthurian onomastics', TRANSACTIONS OF THE HONOURABLE SOCIETY OF CYMMRODORION, 1969, 250–64.

Chapter IX: Was There an Arthur of the Welsh? (pp. 120–9)

Dooley, Ann, and Harry Roe (trans.), TALES OF THE ELDERS OF IRELAND (ACALLAM NA SENÓRACH), Oxford: Oxford University Press, 1999.

Ó hÓgáin, Dáithí, FIONN MAC CUMHAILL. IMAGES OF THE GAELIC HERO, Dublin: Gill and Macmillan, 1988.

Acknowledgements

Several people have helped by discussion and in other ways. I particularly thank Dr Brian Golding, Dr Nerys Ann Jones, Michael Polkinhorn and Professor Brynley Roberts; also several former students, especially Jonathan Coe, Anna Langford and Barry Lewis; and an anonymous reader for the Press; but none of them should be implicated in the views expressed here.

The Author

O. J. Padel is a lecturer in Celtic languages and literature in the Department of Anglo-Saxon, Norse and Celtic (University of Cambridge), and a bye-fellow of Peterhouse. Born and brought up in London, and educated at the Universities of Cambridge and Edinburgh, he has also lived and worked in Aberystwyth and Cornwall. His research is mainly concerned with Cornish place-names, and hence with Cornish language, literature and history at all periods, particularly the Middle Ages; also with the Arthurian legend, especially in Welsh, and with saints and their cults in Celtic countries.

Designed by Jeff Clements
Typesetting at the University of Wales Press in
11pt Palatino and printed in Great Britain by
Dinefwr Press, Llandybïe, 2000

British Library Cataloguing in Publication Data.
A catalogue record for this book is available from the
British Library.

ISBN 0-7083-1682-4 paperback
     0-7083-1689-1 hardback

**The publication of this book has been made possible by
grants from the Eugène Vinaver Fund and from the
Scouloudi Foundation in association with the Institute
of Historical Research (University of London).**